A GARDENER'S GUIDE TO

TULIPS

Ensuring successful cultivation
in the garden

A GARDENER'S GUIDE TO
TULIPS

Ensuring successful cultivation
in the garden

MATTHEW SMITH AND GRETE SMITH

✱ THE CROWOOD PRESS

First published in 2023 by
The Crowood Press Ltd
Ramsbury, Marlborough
Wiltshire SN8 2HR

enquiries@crowood.com

www.crowood.com

British Library Cataloguing-in-Publication Data
A catalogue record for this book is available from the British Library.

ISBN 978 0 7198 4203 0

Cover design by Sergey Tsvetkov

Photo Credits
All photographs are taken by Grete Smith unless otherwise stated. Antsvgdal/Shutterstock.com: p. 164, bottom left; Barmalini/Shutterstock.com: p. 48; Evrenkalinbacak/Shutterstock.com: p. 133; Floralia Brussels, Castle Grand-Bigard: p. 132; John Amand, Jacques Amand Intl: p. 23, bottom, p. 145; John Wainwright: p. 150, bottom; Kelsey Gurnett/Shutterstock.com: p. 153; Dr Liang Guo: pp. 134, 135, top; Martin Duncan, Head Gardener Arundel Castle: pp. 126, 127, 128; PicoStudio/Shutterstock.com: p. 66, top right; Steve Photography/Shutterstock.com: p. 169, bottom; Stocker Plus/Shutterstock.com: p. 162; Teresa Clements: pp. 142, 150, top; Uhryn Larysa/Shutterstock.com: p. 14.
   Google [Google Maps Europe/Asia]. Retrieved 10 January 2022, from https://www.google.co.uk/maps/@43.6123397,40.4405249,4.04z–p. 163;
   Wikimedia Commons – Retired electrician // Map: user:STyx, CC0, *Own work based on figure 1 in Christenhusz, M. et al. Tiptoe through the tulips – cultural history, molecular phylogeetics and classification of Tulipa (Liliaceae) // Botanical Journal of the Linnean Society.* (2013, Vol, 172. pp.280-328)- p. 13.

Acknowledgements
We would like to thank The Crowood Press for making this publication possible. There are many other people who contributed directly and indirectly with information, advice, suggestions and support, and we would particularly like to thank Teresa Clements for generously sharing her knowledge and expertise on the amateur showing of tulips in Chapter 8. Likewise, we would like to thank the Committee and members of the Wakefield and North of England Tulip Society for welcoming us to their show and introducing us to the fascinating world of the English Florists' Tulips. We would like to thank all those who kindly supported us, shared their gardens and additional photography of gardens and spent time speaking to us about the tulips they grow: Dr Ellie McCann, Polly Nicholson, Martin Duncan, Dr Liang Guo, Nicole Pelgrims and Imogen Wyvill.
   Thank you to John Amand from Jacques Amand International for the rare photos of historic tulips and of the photo Lawrence Medal Award Garden from RHS Chelsea Flower Show 1995.
   We are very pleased to have included information from the adoptive country of the tulip, the Netherlands, and that would have not been possible without the help of Simon Groot. Thank you to Joris van der Velden and Adriaan Dekker for talking to us about breeding tulips and growing tulips for cut flowers.
   Last but not least, we would like to thank our families and friends for patiently bearing with us when we disappeared from sight while our chapters were taking shape.

Typeset by Envisage IT
Printed and bound in India by Replika Press Pvt. Ltd.

CONTENTS

FOREWORD

Presumably if you have just bought this book or are thinking of treating yourself to it, you are already interested in tulips. You may very well grow them, perhaps you know quite a bit about them.

Lots of us gardeners grow tulips, love them and are fascinated by them. They are perhaps the most charismatic of flowers. On whatever level you appreciate them, from the elevated heights of their historical significance to the literally down-to-earth level of just planting bulbs in your garden and watching them grow, they mean a great deal to many people.

There is so much to discover about them – where do they come from? How long have gardeners been growing them? How did they come to cause the ruin of a country's economy and centuries later become the cornerstone of that same country's economic success?

There are chapters about how to grow this special bulb. What are the conditions that suit it? Are they best grown on their own? How do we integrate them into our gardens? On a gardening level, you will learn about the types of tulips we can grow, which to choose, and what about the species. And there are sections about how you might make your choices based on colour and flowering period. Can you grow tulips from seed? What about replanting offsets?

How do the Netherlanders grow their tulips so successfully? Their striped tulip fields are visible from space. Years ago, I made a programme entitled *Plant Odysseys* with Oxford Scientific Films for BBC 2. One episode was devoted to 'The Tulip' and in it I was lucky enough to visit the Netherlands' bulb fields. Grete and Matthew let us into this fascinating world. They tell us not only about the techniques and practice of growing tulips but about the graft and patience, the industry and the love that goes into producing our tulip bulbs.

They talk about the Silk Road, where centuries ago merchants and travellers on horseback transported their bulbs on epic, often hazardous journeys westwards through mountainous terrain, thence to the courts of the Turks and the Ottomans and on to the flat fields of the Netherlands, to their tulip-advertising garden at Keukenhof, visited by millions, and to the Aalsmeer flower auction, the fourth largest building by area in the world, where the majority of the world's cut flowers, especially tulips, are bought and sold.

We have insights not only into how tulips are grown commercially, but how they have been grown and developed over the centuries and how we can grow them for ourselves. Expert information about where to see tulips at their best in a variety of venues is included, not just dry data but what special features each venue boasts, illustrated with excellent photographs. When you are writing about any flower, words are brought to life by images and the photographs throughout the book are first rate. Of course the tulip has to be one of the most photogenic of flowers. The images here are mouth-watering.

The book is written by enthusiasts for enthusiasts, bursting with useful facts, informed by first-hand knowledge. You know the authors understand their subject intimately – from growing them and constantly gleaning extra knowledge from fellow enthusiasts. Within these pages you will find comprehensive and brilliantly researched answers to all you want to know about tulips, whether you are planting vast borders or a container or two. For all this information to have been brought together in one volume is a huge achievement. You need look no further except for the fact that reading these pages will inspire you to look even more deeply into this bewitching flower.

Carol Klein, Spring 2023

INTRODUCTION

This book is aimed at keen gardeners as well as budding gardeners interested in ornamental horticulture and, more specifically, in tulip growing. Practical aspects of tulip cultivation including aspects pertaining to the bulb as planting material, planting suggestions, conditions for thriving, tulip varieties and perhaps lesser-known information about cultivating tulips at a larger scale, have been included in the text. While not a central point of this book, we felt it was appropriate also to include a section on the current debate around the place of the tulip in history.

When approached to write this book, we thought of all the different ways in which through Brighter Blooms we have been involved with tulips, aside from growing them. We felt that there is often little printed information about flower shows which, after all, are a very important platform for Brighter Blooms and many other small size growers, and a great opportunity to interact with customers and people with a similar interest in plants and growing. Equally, based on Matthew's experience of speaking to gardening groups and societies, we were aware there is a great appetite for information on public and private places open to the public that display tulips in such a way that excites and inspires visitors. Not only that, but we ourselves value the opportunity to visit, admire and understand the level of endeavour that other commercial tulip growers and amateur tulip enthusiasts invest in presenting tulips at their best to a wider public. The information provided in this book comes not only from our experience as horticulture enthusiasts and keen admirers of gardens in the UK and worldwide, but also from the experience of a small grower of tulips based in the northwest of England with over ten years' experience of growing tulips at our nursery, and displaying at the Royal Horticultural Society (RHS) shows and other independent flower shows.

Each chapter concludes with a case study, which is a place, an aspect, or a variety that we felt we wanted to emphasise as being particularly representative for the topic further developed within the chapter.

In Chapter 1 we talk about the origins – tulips from Amsterdam? being our opening question. We then talk about taxonomy and different types of tulips, and it is this classification that we base the rest of the text on when referring to the different groups of tulips. *Tulipa acuminata* is the first case study, selected as such for being, in our view, a bridge between tulips past and present, an unusual reminder through its appearance of how things change, but at their core, remain appreciated.

Moving on to the practical knowledge of bulbs as planting material and factors we need to bear in mind when planting them, Chapter 2 considers the ideal conditions for bulbs to grow well and tulips to thrive in, and concludes with a very small-scale, unscientific experiment looking at the results of growing different sizes of bulbs. Chapter 3 considers the post-bulb stage of the tulips, namely, the conditions in the garden while they are growing that provide useful growing notes for gardeners. A good understanding of the full life cycle of the tulips helps growers ensure the right conditions are provided and, in return, the best displays are the result they see.

Chapter 4 offers suggestions on including tulips in garden design, alongside a discussion on colour combinations, and includes in the case study a private garden from the northwest as a great example to allow for different colour schemes and planting styles in different parts of the garden successfully.

We then move back to looking at more technical aspects related to tulips and discuss propagation and breeding in Chapter 5, which we conclude with an interview with Joris van der Velden, a Dutch tulip breeder.

Following on from breeding, Chapter 6 is where we list varieties that we have been growing for many years and we invite gardeners who may not have grown them before to consider them. All tulip varieties included in this chapter are varieties that we are happy to recommend to gardeners and tulip enthusiasts for growing.

Back on the road, Chapter 7 includes several destinations in England, Europe and further afield where tulips are expertly grown and beautifully displayed, followed by Chapter 8, where we explore the world of tulips exhibited as part of flower shows in amateur and commercial displays. The only remaining UK tulip society is the case study for Chapter 8.

We thought that writing about tulips would not be complete without referring to the very well-developed tulip cut flower industry in the Netherlands. And while a completely different approach to growing from what has been presented in previous chapters, we felt it would be interesting for readers to find out more about the scale of the tulip cut flower industry. The case study for this chapter is that of a small company based in Hem, in the Netherlands.

Finally, the concluding chapter of this book gives a synopsis of some of the older and newer publications on Tulipmania. There is also a discussion on the known accounts of the story, which has been retold many times.

TULIP ORIGINS, TAXONOMY, TYPES AND CLASSIFICATION

Tulips have been known for over 1,000 years, and it is easy to imagine that within this time span everything that could have been learnt about tulips has been learnt; however, this could not be further from the truth. Taxonomy is the branch of science concerned with classification (Oxford English Dictionary) often through naming, sorting and categorising. The tulip has been subject to extensive taxonomical scrutiny and change, with a vast amount of effort having been put into the classification of the genus over time. As science has developed, our understanding of the tulip

There have been many thousands of hybrids registered since the seventeenth century when the Dutch started cultivating tulips. Tulip 'Verandi' is just one of several thousand registered with the KAVB – the Dutch Bulb Growers' Association.

A species tulip called *Tulipa cretica*. Originating from the isle of Crete. One of over seventy known species of which there are many hundreds of cultivars.

has changed, and this has led to taxonomical reclassification and adjustments to the genus. Even now, work continues to fully understand how the genus should be classified at a genetic level and, while most gardeners will not be concerned with the current thinking on taxonomy or historical classifications, for the readers who are, further reading can be found in the Bibliography section.

In this chapter we will consider the origins of tulip species and their geographical spread. While this may not seem to be a priority, as we will discuss here, the origin of the species lies at the basis of the conditions needed for the respective species to thrive, therefore it has a direct impact on successful cultivation, be it from the point of view of the gardener who grows tulips in their garden, or the designer who proposes where tulips should go in the garden. We will then look more closely at the humble tulip species, the starting point of the impressive tulip hybrids with which we are now familiar. Finally, and having in mind selecting the tulips, rather than focussing closely on the complicated taxonomy of genus and species, we look a little deeper into the current classification of the hybrids as these are more familiar to most gardeners and readers. Making selections based on flower shape, stem length and flowering time can be made easier when the details of tulip categories are known.

TULIPS FROM AMSTERDAM?

When the general population are asked the question, 'Where do tulips come from?' the answer often received from most people is 'Holland', or quite often more specifically, Amsterdam. And why would the answer not be that? After all, there is a song titled 'Tulips from Amsterdam' and the internet has thousands of photos of the Dutch tulip fields. While the answer is not exactly wrong, with approximately 70 per cent of the world's commercial supply of tulip bulbs being grown in the Netherlands, the tulip has no native origins in Holland, or indeed, Western Europe. The fact that so many see Holland as the home of the tulip is certainly a testament to the Dutch horticultural skills that have allowed a small country to corner a huge international market, popularise the genus worldwide

The Netherlands is often cited as the home of the tulip, understandably so when you see the fantastic displays created at Keukenhof gardens. However, no tulip is native to the country or indeed, to Northern and Central Europe.

and become associated with the masterfully cultivated tulip.

One of the first things to establish is the fact that there are no tulip species that are native to Central and Northern Europe. The difference between a native and a naturalised plant is that a plant that is naturalised is one that has been brought to an area with human assistance, whereas a native plant originates from that location.

The tulip originally had a quite narrow geographical spread. The most diverse cluster of native tulips is found in the Tien Shan and Pamir-Alay mountain ranges in Central Asia. Taxonomists generally believe that this is the area where the tulip first appeared. Uzbekistan alone has twenty species native to the country. The native tulip populations then form a band between

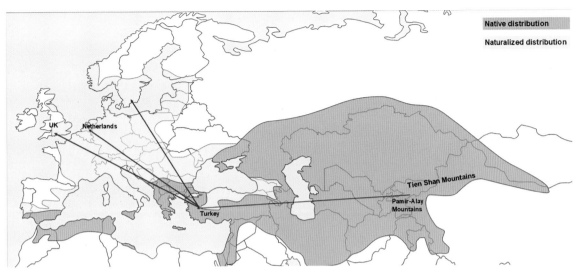

Map showing the native and naturalised distribution of tulips. The mountain ranges represent the area where the largest diversity of tulip species is found. The red lines indicate an approximate widening distribution over time.

western China, Mongolia and the Himalayas in the east. The Balkans are often said to form the most western extent of the native spread of the tulip, although there is one species found to be native to southern Portugal, Spain and North Africa. The band spreads no further north than southern Ukraine and central Siberia and no further south than Egypt, Iraq and Iran.

The tulip has been naturalised in many locations around the world, and across a very long period of time, leading to a situation where establishing whether tulip species are native or naturalised can be a difficult task for researchers. Most of Europe, including as far north as Norway, Finland and Scotland has naturalised colonies of tulips with the most common species being *Tulipa sylvestris*. The naturalised spread of the tulip is very much linked to the historical spread of the tulip and is expanded on in Chapter 10 – History. Fifteen or so varieties have been identified growing wild in Turkey and are considered naturalised. It would appear, however, that only four of them are native to Turkey.

It is worth noting at this point and bearing in mind the growing conditions of the locations where the largest diversity of tulip species is found. Tulips are found growing in mountain ranges in some very inhospitable and remote locations, often extremely cold and wet in the winter and hot and dry in the summer. This is important, as conditions from the place of origin will influence the growing conditions

Tulipa sylvestris is a species tulip with quite a large native spread (Central Asia – Northern Africa) that has successfully naturalised in many locations through Central and Northern Europe. It grows well in grassy meadows and deciduous woodlands.

Species tulip growing in the Chimgan mountains in Uzbekistan.

needed to thrive, even when the original species have been hybridised. The tulips grown in parks and gardens nowadays bear little resemblance to the species native to the slopes of the Tien-Shan mountain range; however, they require similar growing conditions as the species to thrive.

TULIP SPECIES

Originally small, generally low growing with modest flowers, tulip species bear only a slight resemblance to the modern-day hybrids that most of us think of when we talk about tulips. Most tulip species have pointy petals which can be described as somewhat thinner in texture than the petals of the tulip hybrids. The colour ranges are more limited, with pink, yellow, lilac, purple and orange being the colours most associated with tulip species. While tulip species may not have quite the opulence, stature and presence of the hybrids, they are nevertheless highly collectable among the tulip enthusiasts community and, if the correct growing conditions are available, they will provide a display year

after year, sometimes being considered more reliable as a grouping of tulips at reflowering than the tulip hybrids.

The number of recorded species of tulips is subject to some debate with some papers documenting as many as 114 and others around the seventy-five mark. The problem of pinpointing an exact number is down to the variability within the species. The breeding of varieties within species and varieties documented as species that have never, as far as we know, been located within the wild has added to the confusion. A species in one part of the globe can look and grow very differently to one established elsewhere. If all species are eventually DNA sequenced, then an exact number of species will be decided upon. Until then, however, there will continue to be much debate on this subject. The seventy-five plus species documented do have quite a variation and we do not have space in this book to document every one of them. Richard Wilford's book *Tulips, Species and Hybrids for the Gardener* (2006) is a great publication which describes some of the more well-known, cultivated and commercially available species and varieties.

To the general gardener much of the species debate is inconsequential, and whether or not they can be grown in the garden is the most important aspect. Some of the species do indeed require very specific growing conditions, often liking very dry or cold conditions at specific times of the year. The intolerance to wet conditions means these species tend only to be suitable for managed cultivation in glasshouse growing. Apart from those requiring specific conditions, on the whole, most species require free-draining soils; silty loam soils are perfect, heavy clay soils are not ideal. However, *Tulipa turkestanica* has been known to grow in a wide range of conditions and will even survive on heavier soils. Tulips are best grown in open, light sunny locations. The following three varieties lend themselves to growing in garden situations.

Tulipa turkestanica

Tulipa turkestanica grows with a few narrow grey-green leaves. Flowering In early April, flowers are creamy-white with a yellow centre and star shaped when open, growing to a height of around 25cm (10in). A single bulb will often have five or more flowers so a well-established, dense clump can be quite a sight. *Tulipa turkestanica* is very tolerant of a range of conditions including heavier soils so long as they do not stay waterlogged, making it one of the easiest of the species tulips to grow and multiply well over time. Its height means it sits well in the flower border without getting lost among other early spring flowers. The early flowers of *Tulipa turkestanica* are often covered in bees on sunny spring days.

Tulipa tarda

Tulipa tarda usually flowers after *Tulipa turkestanica*, and grows low to the ground, to approximately 15cm (6in). It produces star-shaped flowers which are intense yellow in the centre and white around the tip and the exterior top part of the petals, a colour combination which makes *Tulipa tarda* glisten in the early spring sunshine. The foliage is relatively insignificant with thin, linear green leaves surrounding the flowers, which emerge centrally. When planted in dense clusters, *Tulipa tarda* produces great splashes of early colour to gardens. *Tulipa tarda* was assigned the Award of Garden Merit by the RHS in 2015.

Tulipa humilis

Tulipa humilis is a species that has numerous varieties in cultivation which we feel gardeners should consider, due to its versatility and reliability. The original *Tulipa humilis* is of a lilac colour, with the interior centre of the flower yellow. Most other varieties pertaining to this species retain the yellow centre, but many are more intense in colour. Varieties such as 'Persian Pearl', 'Little Beauty' and 'Little Princess' perform very well in gardens, in sunny, well-drained locations where they multiply freely.

Tulipa turkestanica is a species tulip that will tolerate slightly damper but not waterlogged soils.

Species tulip *Tulipa tarda* works well planted in rockeries or right at the front of well-drained flower beds.

Tulipa humilis has many cultivars that grow very well in sunny, free-draining garden areas. The true species is rarely grown, as its cultivars have a broader appeal.

HYBRID TULIPS – CURRENT TYPES AND CLASSIFICATION SYSTEM

Tulips have been grown, bred, described and classified for hundreds of years, and many books have been published detailing links between historical developments and classifications. For all plant species that have been subjected to extensive breeding over a long period of time, classification systems have been adapted and altered over the years. Tulips are no different. The current classification arose out of a need to organise the vast number of new varieties that had been bred at the end of the nineteenth century. Nomenclature at the time was also very confused, with many of the new varieties being given names that were already in use for a different variety. In 1913 the Royal Horticultural Society (RHS) decided to address this issue by creating a Tulip Nomenclature Committee with the task to establish a classification scheme and resolve the overlap in names. Tulip trials were established at Wisley Gardens during 1914 and 1915 and a final report was published in 1917.

The following fifty years saw a tremendous amount of work into further classifying and renaming tulip varieties. Many subgroups or divisions were discussed at that time, including Broken Breeder Tulips, Mendel Tulips and Cottage Tulips, the latter being a subdivision dropped a long time ago, but which is still mentioned occasionally today. By the 1960s there were twenty-three different subdivisions listed in the tulip classification system, and in 1967 it was decided that a complete overhaul of the system was needed again. Consequently, the subdivisions were changed leading to a reduction of just fifteen subdivisions. Between the first RHS publication – 'A Tentative list of Tulip Names' in 1929 and the last paper publication by the Dutch Royal General Bulb Growers Association – 'Classified List and International Register of Tulip Names' in 1996, which had a supplement published in 2005, there have been fourteen editions of an official tulip list. These have been produced to assist both the horticultural industry and keen gardeners with correct names and specific information for each variety, such as flowering class or type, colour and height.

A good use of creative, if not descriptive naming, Tulip 'Hotpants' and Tulip 'Healthcare'.

The 1996 'Classified List and International Register of Tulip Names' was the last official paper publication, although in 2005 the long-awaited supplement was published (in Dutch mainly) that contained approximately 1,500 new tulip cultivars, updates and corrections that had occurred since 1996. The 1996 edition contains over 5,600 tulip names, of which 2,600 were in cultivation at the time and in most cases readily available to the trade and consumer, according to the preface. The 1996 edition includes all the cultivars in the 1987 edition plus all the new cultivars since 1987. The edition also tries to correct some of the duplicated naming that was created by the practice of reusing names after a few years of cultivars not being seen in commercial production – a practice now frowned upon. This, we assume, has led to some of the inventive names we see nowadays –Tulip Hotpants, for example. Naming of tulips has always been down to the breeder of the variety, with some named varieties gaining popularity through associations. Tulip

Varieties with people's names often have significance with individuals, making them popular choices, Tulip 'Shirley' being a case in point.

Rococo, for instance, is aptly named after the elaborate art style.

Since the last paper supplement in 2005, the Dutch Royal General Bulb Growers Association has overhauled its website to allow for new tulip varieties to be registered, catalogued and updated online. This change is a much welcome one, as the list is now always up to date and can be searched electronically. Today we have a tulip classification list that contains fourteen subdivisions, or fifteen if the Miscellaneous group is included. The Miscellaneous section is not a cultivar group, but is used to cover the entirety of the wild species and their cultivars that do not have a place in the fourteen groups. As breeding continues, new and interesting varieties emerge that blur the boundaries of the groups. For example, which group should Tulip Exotic Emperor

Tulip 'Green Mile' crosses three group boundaries: officially registered as a lily-flowered tulip, it could quite easily be classed as a Viridiflora or a fringed tulip.

A new group of tulips yet to be classified by the Dutch Bulb Growers' Association, Coronet tulips have distinctly pinched petals, making them look like a crown. Top to bottom: Tulip 'Red Dress', Tulip 'Striped Crown' and Tulip 'Elegant Crown'.

feature in? It is both a double and a Fosteriana tulip. The same could be said for Tulip Green Mile, which is registered a lily-flowered tulip, but displays very prominent green marking as categorised in the Viridiflora group and also has fringed edges. There is further an argument that the current list is ready to be augmented with an additional tulip group – the Coronet (or Crown) group. Unlike other groups, tulips from the Coronet group have a very distinctive appearance, with the tips of the petals giving the impression of having been pinched, thus creating a crown-shaped flower. Tulips from the Coronet group are also described as having a much firmer texture than other varieties.

We have included this classification for tulips in our book, as we think it is important to be aware of particularities of tulips that belong to the same grouping, this classification providing gardeners with an easy way to distinguish between tulips in terms of flowering time, petal or flower shape or flower opening habit. The groupings that different varieties fall under are included in information available when purchasing the bulbs and are a very helpful shorthand for busy gardeners. The classification of cultivars in *Tulipa* (1996 'Classified List and international Register of Tulip Names', Royal General Bulb Growers' Association KAVB) is detailed next, together with examples of varieties in each grouping and further explanation where necessary. Most of the varieties we have included here are commercially available and we have grown them on our nursery for many years. Further examples are provided in Chapter 6, with additional information for each variety.

Single Early Group

Single-flowered cultivars, mainly short stemmed and early flowering.

The early nature of this group means that some of these varieties can be the longest lasting; they flower when the sun is still weak and the days are a little shorter. The shorter stems also make them a great addition to the flower border, especially on windier sites. Often used in the forcing trade for very early cut flower tulips.

Varieties: Tulip Flair; Tulip Christmas Dream; Tulip Purple Prince.

Double Early Group

Double-flowered cultivars, mainly short stemmed and early flowering.

Fully doubled flowers that tend to last a long time without getting top heavy like some of the longer stemmed later varieties. A good range of colours is now available.

Varieties: Tulip Abba; Tulip Monsella; Tulip Foxtrot.

Examples of Single Early Group varieties. Left to right: Tulip 'Flair', Tulip 'Christmas Dream' and Tulip 'Purple Prince'.

Examples of Double Early Group varieties. Left to right: Tulip 'Abba', Tulip 'Monsella' and Tulip 'Foxtrot'.

Triumph Group

Single-flowered cultivars, stem of medium length, mid-season flowering. Originally the result of hybridisation between cultivars of the Single Early Group and the Single Late Group.

This group contains by far the largest number of varieties. A lot of varieties being bred currently are for the cut flower industry and this group is favoured amongst the cut flower growers. The medium stem length makes them a popular choice in the garden.

Varieties: Tulip Jimmy; Tulip Abu Hassan; Tulip Don Quichotte.

Darwin Hybrid Group

Single-flowered cultivars, long stemmed, mid-season flowering. Originally the result of hybridisation between cultivars of the Darwin Group with *Tulipa fosteriana* and the result of hybridisation between other cultivars and botanical tulips, which have the same habit and in which the wild plant is not evident.

These hybrids are a relatively new development in the tulip's long history and are a welcome addition to the garden. They are very good for perennial displays as they show a good ability to reappear year after year in the right conditions. With tall stems and large flowers,

Examples of Triumph Group varieties. Left to right: Tulip 'Jimmy', Tulip 'Abu Hassan' and Tulip 'Don Quichotte'.

Examples of Darwin Hybrid Group varieties. Left to right: Tulip 'Mystic van Eijk', Tulip 'Blushing Apeldoorn' and Tulip 'Triple A'.

they can be used to good effect in the flower border and are often seen mass planted in public spaces and parks.

Varieties: Tulip Mystic Van Eijk; Tulip Blushing Apeldoorn; Tulip Triple A.

Single Late Group

Single-flowered cultivars, mainly long stemmed, late flowering. This group includes, for example, the former Darwin Group and Cottage Group.

Extending the flowering season into May, this group may not always be the longest lasting. Some of the cultivars in this grouping include the modern non-virused flamed and feathered varieties.

Varieties: Tulip Queen of Night; Tulip Atlantis; Tulip World Expression.

Lily-flowered Group

Single-flowered cultivars, mid-season or late flowering, flowers with pointed reflexed tepals. Stem of variable length.

Many of the varieties in this group have a distinguishable slender flower shape with pointed petals when compared to tulips from other groups, giving them an elegant stature. As far as we know there are no double lily-flowered tulips currently available.

Varieties: Tulip Ballerina; Tulip White Triumphator; Tulip Aladdin.

Examples of Single Late Group varieties. Left to right: Tulip 'Queen of Night', Tulip 'Atlantis' and Tulip 'World Expression'.

Examples of Lily-flowered Group varieties. Left to right: Tulip 'Ballerina', Tulip 'White Triumphator' and Tulip 'Aladdin'.

Fringed Group

Single-flowered cultivars, tepals are edged with crystal-shaped fringes, mid-season or late flowering. Stem of variable length.

The tulips in this group have petal edges that are frilly or fringed to variable degrees, some so much that they seem aggressively spiked. The Fringed group are often referred to as 'Crispa' in Dutch. Double Fringed tulips have been bred in recent years and are now available commercially.

Varieties: Tulip Crystal Star; Tulip Versaci; Tulip Curly Sue.

Viridiflora Group

Single-flowered cultivars with partly greenish tepals. Late flowering. Stem of variable length.

Viridi translates as green and *flora* as flower. Often just a line of green in the centre of a coloured petal, sometimes a more widespread green flushing on the petals, there is, however, the odd variety that is nearly green. There are several varieties that have green in the petals but have been classified into other groupings.

Varieties: Tulip Flaming Spring Green, Tulip Greenland; Tulip Twilight Princess.

Examples of Fringed Group varieties. Left to right: Tulip 'Crystal Star', Tulip 'Versaci' and Tulip 'Curly Sue'.

Examples of Viridiflora Group varieties. Left to right: Tulip 'Flaming Spring Green', Tulip 'Greenland' and Tulip 'Twilight Princess'.

Rembrandt Group

Cultivars with broken flowers, striped or marked brown, bronze, black, red, pink or purple on red, white or yellow ground, caused by virus infection. Long stemmed. (Not commercially available, only in historic collections.)

Hortus Bulborum in Limmen, Netherlands maintains a historic collection of tulip varieties including many of the broken types much sought after during Tulipmania. Occasionally, small quantities of these varieties can be purchased. The Wakefield and North of England Tulip Society (WNETS) maintains a collection of broken tulips in its members' gardens and allotments. Rather than bulbs being sold, the sharing of bulbs amongst fellow members is encouraged to ensure the collection is not lost.

Often, modern tulips that are clean of virus but have flamed and feathered markings are given this title, which can lead to some confusion.

Varieties: Tulip Absalon, Tulip Black and White, Tulip Saskia.

Examples of Rembrandt Group varieties. Left to right: Tulip 'Absalon', Tulip 'Black and White' and Tulip 'Saskia'.

Parrot Group

Single-flowered cultivars with laciniate, curled and twisted tepals. Mainly late flowering. Stem of variable length.

These could be considered the furthest removed cultivars from the species, and some of the varieties could be mistaken for being virused or diseased. However, all the contortions and colour mottling are a result of breeding. They are certainly a talking point, especially now that double parrots are available.

Varieties: Tulip Rococo; Tulip White Rebel; Tulip Black Parrot.

Double Late Group

Double-flowered cultivars. Late flowering. Mainly long stemmed.

The flowers are often very full, giving the resemblance of frilly peony flowers, hence often being given the name 'peony-flowered tulips'. They are well suited as cut flowers and in flower arranging. Flowering later in the season, double-flowered tulips do not always last that long in flower if the spring weather is warm.

Varieties: Tulip Blue Diamond; Tulip Carnival de Nice; Tulip Gold Fever.

Examples of Parrot Group varieties. Left to right: Tulip 'Rococo', Tulip 'White Rebel' and Tulip 'Black Parrot'.

Examples of Double Late Group varieties. Left to right: Tulip 'Blue Diamond', Tulip 'Carnival de Nice' and Tulip 'Gold Fever'.

Kaufmanniana Group

Tulipa kaufmanniana with her cultivars, subspecies, varieties and hybrids, which resemble *T. kaufmanniana*. Very early flowering, sometimes with mottled foliage. Flower with multicoloured base opens fully. Exterior normally with a clear carmine blush. Height up to 20cm (8in).

Many of the varieties in this classification have flowers that open up fully, giving them the look of a waterlily flower and thus many commercial catalogues contain a section on waterlily tulips. Planted en masse, these varieties are quite dramatic when fully open in the sunshine.

Varieties: Tulip Giuseppe Verdi; Tulip Scarlet Baby; Tulip Stresa.

Fosteriana Group

Tulipa fosteriana with her cultivars, subspecies, varieties and hybrids, which resemble *T. fosteriana*. Early flowering, leaves very broad, green or grey green, sometimes mottled or striped. Stem medium to long. Large long flower, base variable.

Due to the close connection to the species, tulips in the Fosteriana group are very good at naturalising and readily come back year after year in the ground. They were once grouped together as 'Emperor Tulips', presumably due to their large flower size.

Varieties: Tulip Exotic Emperor; Tulip Orange emperor; Tulip Purissima.

Examples of Kaufmanniana Group varieties. Left to right: Tulip 'Giuseppe Verdi', Tulip 'Scarlet Baby' and Tulip 'Stresa'.

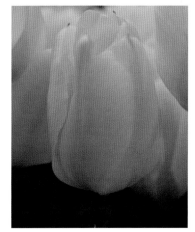

Examples of Fosteriana Group varieties. Left to right: Tulip 'Exotic Emperor', Tulip 'Orange Brilliant' and Tulip 'Purissima'.

Greigii Group

Tulipa greigii with her cultivars, subspecies, varieties and hybrids, which resemble *T. greigii*. Mostly with mottled or striped foliage, flowering later than *kaufmanniana*. Leaves spreading normally on the ground, mostly strongly undulated. Flower shape variable.

The generally short stature of this group makes them particularly well suited to rockeries, containers and fronts of borders. They are often combined with the Kaufmanniana group in catalogues to form a rockery category.

Varieties: Tulip Pinocchio; Tulip Winnipeg; Tulip Toronto.

Miscellaneous

In fact not a cultivar group, but the collection of all species, varieties and their cultivars in which the wild species is evident, not belonging to any of the above-mentioned cultivars groups.

There is some debate about the exact number of species, but there are seventy-five as a minimum. When varieties and cultivars of the species are taken into account, it runs to many hundreds. Some of the species require very specific growing conditions, which are generally replicated in glasshouses; however, numerous varieties can be grown in a garden setting.

Varieties: *Tulipa humilis*; *Tulipa sylvestris*; *Tulipa clusiana*.

Examples of Greigii Group varieties. Left to right: Tulip 'Pinocchio', Tulip 'Winnipeg' and Tulip 'Toronto'.

Examples of Miscellaneous Group varieties. Left to right: *Tulipa humilis* 'Little Beauty', *Tulipa sylvestris* and *Tulipa clusiana cashmeriana*.

CHAPTER 1 CASE STUDY

Tulipa acuminata

We have chosen *Tulipa acuminata* as our case study here as it is quite unique both in appearance and status within the classification. *Tulipa acuminata* also represents an almost lost genetic link to the Ottoman tulip varieties from long ago.

Tulipa acuminata was first named in 1813 and described as a species tulip by Danish-Norwegian botanist Martin Vahl. However, it has never been identified in the wild and, in all likelihood, is a hybrid that potentially dates back to the Ottoman era. *Tulipa acuminata* resembles some of the tulips represented in Ottoman era historic artefacts such as tiles and pottery from the seventeenth century. *Tulipa acuminata* represents the style of tulip the sultans at the time were striving for. The Ottoman tulip breeders and collectors favoured as narrow a petal as possible, often describing them as 'needles'. The only varieties apart from *Tulipa acuminata* that may be considered to come close today are some from the lily-flowered group with more slender and elongated petals, but even those are not comparable. Why this particular variety survived the changing preference from the Ottoman empire times to the bowl-shaped flowers of Tulipmania and beyond favoured by the Western world, we do not know. However, we feel that *Tulipa acuminata* is certainly worth growing to get a glimpse back into historical trends, and to add to the multitude of shapes of tulip flowers in the garden.

Tulipa acuminata will grow to a height of 40–50cm (16–20in) in full sun or partial shade in any good-quality soil. Like other tulips, it is fully hardy and will tolerate being left in the ground during the summer as long as the soil is free draining. The flower colour of *Tulipa acuminata* can be very variable in nature and include yellow mixed in with the red of the petals to various degrees. The narrow petals are prone to twisting in the sunshine, giving the flowers a somewhat contorted appearance but, at the

Tulipa acuminata – an unusual tulip with long, narrow pointed petals, similar in style to the tulips sought after by the Ottomans in the sixteenth and seventeenth centuries.

same time, an exotic appearance reminiscent of an oriental symbol. This is also the reason why *Tulipa acuminata* is also referred to as the 'horned' tulip. Similarly to the flowers, the leaves are also a lot narrower than modern-day hybrids, with a pronounced undulation of the edge of the leaves, with the leaves of *Tulipa acuminata* more closely resembling the leaves of some of the species.

Tulipa acuminata can be grown as a clump in the border but probably lends itself better to drift planting with other varieties, or under-planted below low shrubs where it can show off its uniqueness in isolation. It will grow perfectly well in containers and should be treated like the other hybrids; however, mixing with other varieties when planted is likely to give equally aesthetically satisfying results as it would if planted on its own.

THE BULBS AND PLANTING

Show visitors and customers often ask us if tulips are perennial and if they are hardy. It sometimes transpires in conversation that there is some confusion over tulips being hardy or perennial. We felt this chapter was a good place to start with the explanation. A perennial plant is a plant which lives longer than two years. Many perennial plants include a dormancy period during their yearly life cycle, and that applies to tulips; following blooming in the spring, the regrowth of an entirely new bulb and formation of bulblets throughout the summer season, the foliage withers away and the bulbs are the part of the plant that remains alive and are the starting point for next year's tulips. As discussed later in this chapter, some gardeners prefer to replace and renew tulip displays every year, and so they clear the site of any bulbs from the previous growing season. But naturalised tulips, as those in our experimental tulip bed demonstrate, are perennial plants, as they are not replaced and return to flowering year after year. Hardiness is the plants' ability to stay alive throughout winter temperatures. There are different degrees of hardiness, but the origin of tulips on high Asian mountain slopes suggests significant hardiness. In addition, the presence of glycol in the bulbs acts as an anti-freeze, making tulips suitable for growing in the coldest Northern European winter conditions.

TULIP BULBS

Like most other plants, tulips produce seeds and they can be multiplied using the seed. There are, however, several reasons as to why growing from bulbs is the preferred method. We will discuss growing from seed in more depth in Chapter 5, but this is a good point at which to explain the benefits for growing tulips from bulbs. Firstly, by starting with a bulb, which is a type of vegetative reproduction, most of the plant already exists, but in a dormant stage. As explained below, a flower bud is present inside each bulb of a certain size, and the basal stem (or basal plate) allows the root system to start developing in a vigorous manner as soon as the bulb is placed in soil and can access moisture. This means that by planting bulbs in autumn, we are guaranteed a flower display in spring. The same would not be the case if sowing tulip seeds.

More importantly, the vegetative reproduction, which is based on meristematic cell division, means that cells or tissue from one plant can be induced to grow, producing a clone, or an identical plant to that which provided the cells or tissue. Another good example of vegetative reproduction is propagation by cuttings, where the same principle applies to a different part of the plant. What this means is that the new plant will be true to its origin, therefore making this

Tulip bulbs are the dormant stage in the tulip plant's life cycle. This stage makes the job of lifting and transplanting a tulip plant very easy, as there is no top growth to damage.

Tulip bulbs planted in late autumn will have developed vigorous white roots by mid-winter. Leaves will then develop through late winter and early spring, followed by the elongation of flower stems and buds as spring progresses. Buds will then colour and eventually burst into flower in spring.

The hot summers initiate flower bud formation then the cold weather after planting causes bulbs to emerge out of dormancy and commence the growing season. When planted in the ground or in containers, in the first instance the root system will develop and strengthen. Then the leaves will start forming and the stem will elongate, with the final stage being the bud gradually changing colour and then flowering.

Bulb size

Most people would probably not give a second thought to the size of the bulbs they are buying, unless they saw two different sizes beside each other. In all likelihood, they would then pick the larger ones, which at first glance would be the obvious choice. However, there is more to consider than 'bigger is better'.

When propagating naturally, four to five small, mini-bulblets are formed at the base of each main bulb, near the basal stem. These bulblets must grow to a certain size before flowers are seen; they will not produce flowers in the first few years of growth. More will be explained about the mini-bulblets in Chapter 5 – Propagation and Breeding. When tulip bulbs grown commercially are lifted, they get graded into different sizes from the small bulblets through to the larger sizes. Historically, this was done by hand using grading

method most successful for continuing the cultivation of specific varieties and cultivars. Unlike using bulbs as the planting material, growing from seeds is unlikely to produce a flower similar to that produced by the mother plant. In addition, it may take four to seven years for flowers to be produced if propagating from seed, which often exceeds the patience of the keenest gardeners.

Bulbs are essentially a modified plant, with the bulb stage within the life cycle of the plant allowing the plant to survive through a period of dormancy. True bulbs like tulips store all their growing parts and enough nutrient to survive and re-emerge from that dormancy. The need for dormancy can be for many reasons, but in the case of tulips it is to survive the hot dry summers that occur in their native locations.

A tulip bulb with bulblets around the base, which have developed in the first year after planting. They will all be too small to flower initially but could be grown on for a year or two until they reach flowering size.

Even without grading cards and machines the difference between bulb sizes is perfectly apparent when they are placed together. All these will flower in the first year after planting, but in theory, the larger bulbs will produce a larger flower; *see* case study further in this chapter.

cards or, when skilled enough, by eye. Today all grading is mechanised with minimal human input. The measurements used for grading refer to the circumference of the bulb. The smaller bulblets and bulbs too small to flower are set aside for replanting. The larger ones are made available for sale. Generally, the bulbs available from garden centres, flower shows and online websites have three standard sizes, referring to the circumference of the bulb: 9–10cm (3½–4in), 10–11cm (4–4½in) and 12cm+ (5in+). A 10–11cm (4–4½in) bulb has a circumference of approximately the size of a plastic milk bottle top. The exception to these standard measures are species tulips, which do

not get as large as the hybrid bulbs that are most commonly sold. Sometimes smaller size bulbs are available for sale (8–9cm/3–3½in), which will not produce a satisfactory flower. The larger size bulbs (14cm+/5½in+), when available, are often used for growing for exhibitions and competitions. True species tulips are generally available in sizes 4–5cm (1½–2in).

As a general rule, once the bulb reaches flowering size, the size of the bulb dictates the size of the flower, hence the bigger the bulb we plant, the larger the flower it is likely to produce. So why sell different sizes and not just the biggest? One reason is cost, as the bigger bulbs are more expensive. They may well take an extra year of growing to produce and therefore cost more. Even if they do not take longer the grade out of bigger bulbs, or the separated proportion of bigger

These rockery tulips are grown from 9–10cm (3½–4in) bulbs and produce a perfectly acceptable display especially when grown en masse.

bulbs will be less and therefore the supply and demand dynamics drives the price higher for larger bulbs. Mass-planted flower beds will look just as impressive planted with 10–11cm (4–4½in) bulbs as with the larger 12cm+ (5in+) bulbs and the savings will be significant.

Even if cost was no object to the customer, buying the biggest might still not always be the best option. Take a windy site, for example; if we plant large bulbs and get large flowers they are more likely to get damaged by the wind than smaller flowers from smaller bulbs. Shorter Greigii and Kaufmanniana types flower with a very reasonable-sized flower even at 9–10cm (3½–4in) and, given they are often used on rockeries and at the front of borders, an oversized flower head with a very short stem close to the ground could potentially look somewhat out of proportion.

Larger bulbs certainly have their place and have a fantastic display potential when planted as a small clump in the flower border. They work particularly well if individual bulbs are drifted through a border with the aim of them punctuating deciduous shrubs in the spring. If funds allow, investing in the largest bulbs for container displays is worthwhile. 'Bigger is better' for these features.

Bulb appearance inside and out

The outer layer of the bulb has a papery texture and it is known as the bulb tunic. It offers some protection to the inner bulb when lifting, grading and packing takes place in the bulb industry – an added bonus commercially, but not quite what nature designed it for. The real role of the tunic is to protect the bulb from drying out during the long, warm summer months whilst the bulb is dormant in the ground. The colour and texture of the tunic can vary quite dramatically, with the tunics of some tulip varieties being very delicate and often detaching themselves from the rest of the bulb during the storage period, and others remaining firmly attached and presenting a rougher, more substantial texture. One such variety which is relatively easy to recognise from the bulb and the tunic appearance is *Tulipa praestans* 'Fusilier'. The thicker dark brown outer is similar to the tunics found on most species tulips and rarely falls off.

Inside, layers of individual white, fleshy scales cover the flower bud, which has formed during the warm summer months. A tulip bulb needs approximately eight weeks of temperatures above 18°C but not more than 28°C for a flower bud to form correctly. The fleshy

When planting containers, using the largest bulb size possible (12cm+/5in+ if budget allows) gives the best results.

Tulip bulbs with different-coloured tunics; the darker coloured bulbs in the middle row are the very recognizable *Tulipa praestans* types.

Here you can see a tulip bulb that has been cut straight down the centre. The fleshy scales that will become leaves are clearly visible.

Most tulips grow a single stem and flower from one bulb; however, there are a few varieties that produce multiple stems from a bulb. Tulip 'Scarlet Baby' is a good example.

Tulip 'Antoinette', a fine example of a multi-headed tulip. Rather than a single flower, multiple flowers are held on a single stem.

scales, which will form into leaves, are attached at the base of the tulip by a basal plate, which is where the roots will grow from. Most tulip bulbs produce a singular stem, although there are a number of multi-headed and multi-stemmed tulip varieties. A multi-headed variety will have one stem, which will then branch to form two or three flowering heads as opposed to a multi-stemmed variety where from one bulb three individual stems emerge, each of them possessing a single flower.

Bulb quality

The general appearance of bulbs will provide good clues as to their quality. The main aspect to look for is firmness. If bulbs are firm, relatively heavy and feel turgescent, this indicates that they are healthy and suitable for planting. Ideally, the papery tunic will be complete and reasonably well attached to the bulb, as this will have prevented the bulb from drying out. However, it is not essential as some varieties very readily shed their tunic. Where a tunic is damaged or gone, a closer inspection of the bulb is worthwhile to check

The bulbs in this photo do not have clean, attractive looking tunics. Deep pitting on bulbs should be treated with caution as their successful growth could be compromised. Always buy bulbs that look good and feel firm.

that the fleshy scales have not dehydrated or been damaged. If they are crisp, hollow, powdery, lacking weight and turgidity or the flesh shows large areas of browning, the chances of them growing well or at all are limited. It is not uncommon, depending on storage conditions, to observe small spots of mould developing. These moulds usually develop because of environmental factors – usually a lack of air flow. If these are very small or negligible, easily wiped off and the bulb continues to feel firm, then the chances are it will still be suitable for planting.

Interestingly, we have noted some of the earliest varieties, such as Tulip Heart's Delight can be prone to acquiring blemishes during the storage period, which become most apparent in the period before planting. The blemishes appear on the exterior scales following the tunic disintegrating. Often, the blemishes look like small brown marks and, although somewhat unsightly, they do not impact on the quality of the leaves or flowers as they are protected by several layers of scales. It is always worth examining the basal stem part of the bulb, which is where the root system develops from. Soft rot often manifests itself through softness around the basal stem area; the base should feel firm to the push. Mouldy growth around the basal stem is a sure sign the bulb is compromised.

In order to avoid blemishes and rots developing, the optimum storage conditions for the bulbs are in dry, cool and well-ventilated locations. Commercially, they will be stored in wire net-bottomed wooden trays or specialist plastic bulbs crates, often with air blown over or through them. At home it is best to store bulb in nets or open trays to allow air flow and avoid condensation.

Dutch wire net trays are used commercially to allow good air flow around the bulbs while they are stored. At home, any open tray or net would work well. If stored in closed boxes, checking for moisture among the bulbs periodically is advisable.

They can be kept in paper bags or cardboard boxes, but be aware even these can sometimes cause condensation to form, often referred to as 'sweating'. Plastic packing is slowly being phased out and replaced with biodegradable plastic alternatives, but bulbs should still be removed from these as soon as possible to prevent sweating.

Planting tulip bulbs

Best planting time

Although tulip bulbs are available to buy from August onwards and keen gardeners like to be very organised with their autumn planting material, it is recommended that tulip bulbs are not planted until the soil

Tulip fire is a fungal disease that affects both foliage and flowers, causing unsightly browning and contorting on petals. Further information can be found in Chapter 3.

temperatures have lowered considerably. There are two reasons for this: firstly, the dormancy is broken by cold weather, and planting too early could result in the bulbs not necessarily growing much. This leaves them vulnerable to attacks from pests, usually of the sharp teeth type – mice and squirrels. Tulips are one of the few bulbs that root readily in cold weather, unlike daffodils or crocus, which need the warmer soils late summer/early autumn to root and 'settle in' before the colder months of winter.

Secondly, the lower temperature of the soil means that the preponderance of various diseases harboured in the soil, particularly fungal diseases such as tulip fire, has lowered, therefore offering safer growing conditions. Ideally, the soil temperatures will be below 12 or 13°C. It is fine to plant in October if the soils have started to cool down, but we think November and December are the best months to plant new tulip bulbs, although we have often planted tulip bulbs in January, which flowered successfully in April and May. Tulips need two to three months of cold weather to root properly, so planting at the beginning of the year still gives January, February and March for rooting and growing. However, the danger of waiting is that the ground becomes too frozen to allow for planting and the window for planting is missed all together. An exception to this would be planting in containers where fresh growing media is used. This is discussed in more depth in Chapter 3.

Planting density

The planting density will often depend on several factors, such as the planting environment (direct in the soil, or in containers), the size of the bulbs and the effect we aim to achieve (mass colour, spot planting),

Tulip bulbs can be planted as close as 5 or 6cm (2–2½in) when intended for a one-year bedding display.

When planted as close as this, the results are rather dramatic.

the length of time intended for the display and the tulip type. We could also list financial constraints here; we often speak to landscapers who talk about the budget versus the area to be planted dictating the planting density.

Botanical tulips, for instance, produce smaller bulbs than the decorative hybrids, and mature plants are of a more petite size than their hybrid counterparts. Equally, botanical tulips are significant to a lesser extent for the display they create in terms of colour and vibrancy, and more from the point of view of interest in botany and seeing the closest to the original species that the current hybrids have been bred from. The planting density for botanical tulips would largely depend on the desired display, with 2.5–3.5cm (1–1½in) distance between bulbs being a suitable planting density, although for an intense container display they could be planted with as little as 1cm (½in) separation.

Using the length of time intended for the display criteria, displays can be subdivided into long-term

displays – intended for several years – and non-permanent displays, where bulbs planted the previous year will be removed every year after flowering to make space for a redesign of the garden. A good example of the displays being changed yearly with spectacular effects is provided in the Chapter 7 case study on Keukenhof Gardens.

If using medium-sized bulbs (10–11cm/4–4½in), for a single season display, the planting density to achieve a tight, colourful display can be 6–8cm (2½–3¼in) apart, or up to 200 bulbs per square metre. For the biggest size bulbs (14cm+/5½in+), the planting distance should be increased to 8–10cm (3¼–4in) apart or up to 150 bulbs per square meter. For general planting in the garden for a display intended for several years, planting medium-sized bulbs 12–15cm (4¾–6in) apart (approximately 60–65 bulbs per square metre) will produce a very good display, without being as tight as it would normally be for shows and exhibitions. A very early study from Lincolnshire (1969) showed that flower stem length was influenced by planting density in a proportional fashion: the higher the planting density, the higher the flower stems. In the case of cut flowers, stem length might be of significance. However, within the garden environment it is important to consider factors such as exposure to wind.

In containers, the best visual impact is achieved by applying the tighter planting distances. For a 30 × 30cm (12 × 12in) square container, sixteen bulbs will produce a very good display.

Planting depth

The general, non-scientific rule of thumb when it comes to bulb planting is to plant bulbs twice the depth or height of the bulb. Thus a *Muscari* bulb, which is smaller in size than a tulip bulb at approximately 1.5cm (½in) in height, would need to be planted deep enough for a soil covering of about 3cm (1¼in). Similarly, following this rule, a tulip bulb which may be 4–6cm from base to tip should be planted at a depth of about 8–12cm (3¼–5in).

Similarly to planting density, planting depth is determined by the size of the bulbs and the length of the display. For longer term displays we have found, as has scientific research, a planting depth of 15–20cm (6–8in) to be beneficial for the longevity of successive displays. This is also the case when the intention is to perennialise tulips. While not necessarily planted as mass displays, tulips stand a lot better chance of per-ennialising when bulbs are planted deeper, assuming the soils are not too heavy. For shorter term displays the planting depth can be 10–12cm (4–5in). It is impor-tant to note that, during the growing season, tulip bulbs develop a very vigorous root system, so they will benefit from the availability of good growing soil of a depth of up to 30–40cm (12–16in). In the following chapter, we look at aftercare and whether or not to lift tulip bulbs for the summer dormant period. It is worth noting here that if you intend to lift your tulip bulbs, then planting at 20cm (8in) deep creates a lot of unnecessary work; planting a short-term display at a depth of 10–12cm (4–5in) is advisable.

We have seen research that shows promising results from a shallow planting (5–7.5cm/2–3in) topped with 7.5cm–10cm (3–4in) of mulch to make up the planting depth. This method has various advantages: soils are generally better drained and aerated near the surface, and the mulch provides nutrient to the bulbs as it decomposes. For those who do not like digging, it also reduces the effort of having to dig 20cm (8in) deep holes. We have a raised bed on the nursery that was constructed in a similar way to this, prior to knowledge of the research. We placed tulips at the base of a 20cm (8in) raised bed before filling it with a soil/green waste mix and the results have been very good.

In containers, the depth is important for optimum growing conditions. However, growing in shallow con-tainers is also possible if the moisture of the compost is closely monitored when in a vegetative state and prior to flowering. In containers, the abundant foliage can often obscure very dry compost, so it is important to ensure watering to avoid failings at flowering stage.

Soil types

As with the vast majority of bulbs, tulip bulbs will thrive in well-drained soils which dry out throughout the summer but replenish with moisture in winter

This raised bed has been planted on our nursery for six years. It is planted with Darwin Hybrid tulips, which are well known for good perennialisation. They were planted 20cm (8in) deep and flower reliably year after year with little maintenance.

Tulips planted in heavy, damp or waterlogged soils are unlikely to give a show as good as this in their second year. For best results, plant bulbs in free-draining loam or silty soils.

without becoming waterlogged. Soil types can have a huge effect on how well tulips grow with free-drained soils preferable. In gardens, well-drained, rich, crumbly soils with a neutral to alkaline pH are where tulip bulbs will grow most successfully and longer term. Tulips will, however, grow in a very wide range of soils. Heavier or clay-based soils might allow for one flowering season, but it is unlikely the bulbs will thrive or survive for longer. This is mainly due to the dampness of the heavy soil in the summer not allowing for adequate baking of the bulb. Tulips will, of course, grow in sandy soils but the low nutrient content in these soils can be a problem long term. A good alternative to problematic soils is raised beds, which offer a perfectly apt growing environment if the soil is unsuitable or inaccessible. For containers, good-quality soil-based composts available from horticultural suppliers work very well. A soil-based compost would provide the benefits of being much more suitable for moisture retention, which is a beneficial feature for developing roots and, in addition, they will give containers much more stability than multi-purpose composts would.

The best way to contextualise the optimum growing conditions is to consider growing conditions for the tulip species where they originate from – generally on mountain slopes in fairly poor soil, which get baked in the sun throughout the summer, but get abundant rain and snow during the autumn, winter and spring months. This continuous cycle allows the bulbs to become dormant after they have flowered, in summer, and to restart the vegetative process in winter.

Where in the garden?

The short answer to this question would probably have to be 'somewhere where the tulips can be seen'. Tulips provide the transition between the colour-limited winter season and daffodils, and are followed by the plethora of floral variety offered by late spring and early summer bulbs and herbaceous perennial plants. Tulips are the first explosion of colour in gardens and public spaces, filling places with vibrancy and energy, hence our suggestion that they should be planted where they can be best seen.

Like many of the spring-flowering bulbs, tulips benefit from being planted in a sunny location. If there were flower personality types, we would describe

A fantastic example of mass-planted tulips, here Cardiff Council uses public space to create massive sweeps of Tulip 'Apeldoorn' and Tulip 'Golden Apeldoorn'.

If space allows, large clumps of fifty or more bulbs all the same colour create a statement in the developing herbaceous border. Tulip 'Synaeda Blue'.

tulips as assertive, with a strong presence and always able to stand up for themselves. Thus, if planted in clumps they are best at the fronts or edges of borders, and when mass planted, ample swathes achieve the best effect where space allows. More will be discussed about the visual effects of planting tulips in Chapter 4.

As regards the environmental factors which will enable or inhibit tulips from thriving, light is most definitely an enabler. Not only does light allow the colour and shape of the flowers to stand out, but light can also be responsible for the overall quality of the plant. One particular part which is highly likely to be affected by a lack of sufficient light is the stem. In the correct light conditions, stems tend to be straight and sturdy. Show visitors often ask us what would they need to do to get straight stems when they grow their tulips; and invariably, when they describe the location that yields bent stems, that is a shady spot. The flowers want to access as much light as possible and have the ability to go looking for extra light – which is when the stems become bent. This is linked to the heliotropism, which is the ability of plants to turn and follow the sun's path or direction.

There are downsides to tulips being located in full sun. Many of the tulip varieties have a flower shape which opens wide as a response to light stimulus, and then closes again at night – known as photonastic movement. The repetition of opening wide and closing of the flowers weakens the base of the petals and makes them more susceptible to blow in windy and wet conditions. To extend the optimum display period for tulips, a location which would be north-facing, therefore with no direct sun, but very open and bright could reduce the tendency of flowers to open repeatedly and therefore maintain their strength and last longer.

A good example of the light levels impacting on the length and straightness of the stem, where the bold colour contrast between yellow and black tulips interspersed with blue Muscari does not detract attention from the fact that stems have elongated in their search for light and, with the weight of the flower head, have lost strength and uprightness.

In this example, stems have kept their upright direction because of good light levels, but repeated opening and closing of the flowers has created gaps at the base of the petals, which leave flowers vulnerable to losing their petals in windy conditions.

CHAPTER 2 CASE STUDY

How bulb size affects performance

For most keen gardeners, the joy of gardening comes to a large extent from experimentation. It might be that we see something in someone else's garden, or a place we visit, or on a TV programme. It is to be expected that if we attempt to replicate growing a particular plant, for instance, there is a likelihood that we may get different results if we use a different compost or soil, a different aspect, what it was grown in where we've seen it or apply a different feeding regime. We might not achieve quite the exact same results, or we might find we have done a lot better in our experiment than we expected, or than the example we tried to replicate.

We sourced the sizes discussed in this chapter – 9–10cm (3½–4in), 10–11cm (4–4½in) and 12cm+ (5in+). The difference in bulb size is evident as shown here.

Regardless of the result, it takes nothing away from the excitement of trying something new or experimenting. Like all other keen horticulturalists, we experiment with a wide variety of plants and some of our experiments are more successful than others.

While considering the bulb quality for this chapter, we decided that this would be an eminently suitable opportunity for experimenting with growing different bulb sizes and verifying (or otherwise) the hypothesis that bigger bulbs produce bigger flowers. To establish and illustrate the correlation between the bulb size and the flower size, we decided to conduct an experiment using three popular tulip varieties, in the three different commercially available bulb sizes.

'Flaming Purissima', 'Exotic Emperor' and 'Red Riding Hood' have been chosen for our experiment because of their popularity and wide availability.

For each variety we planted sixteen bulbs in a 30cm (12in) square planter late in the autumn.

The varieties were purposely selected so that they represented different tulip types:

1. Tulip Flaming Purissima
2. Tulip Exotic Emperor
3. Tulip Red Riding Hood

When planting the bulbs, we used the same size containers with the same number of bulbs planted in each container, at a similar depth, as the photographs show. Using the same number of bulbs in a standard container size meant that the planting density differed depending on the size of the bulb. We felt that consistency in method would translate in more credible and replicable results.

As per the photograph, we noted a significant difference between how different varieties performed in our small-scale trial.

An interim survey in the spring showed the Flaming Purissima and Exotic Emperor being far ahead of the Red Riding Hood variety. We noted that best performing bulb size at this particular point was the middle size – 10–11cm (4–4½in) in terms of plant height across the three different varieties.

The Red Riding Hood variety grew very unevenly and unsatisfactorily in each of the different bulb sizes. Having grown this variety in the past without experiencing this problem, we have decided to exclude this variety from the trial to ensure we do not ascribe the variety faults which may be related to the quality of bulbs we sourced for this experiment. The remaining two varieties, Exotic Emperor and Flaming Purissima were monitored at regular intervals.

Exotic Emperor

While a difference in size could be distinguished between the flower size from the 9–10cm (3½–4in) bulbs when compared to 12cm+ (5in+) bulbs, we argue that, as the images show, this difference was not significant, especially when remembering the difference in size of the bulbs.

For this variety, we did, however, notice that the flowers produced by the smaller bulbs matured somewhat slower than the flowers produced by the superior size bulbs, as pictured. Exotic Emperor starts with a buttery colour and it matures to bright white.

It proved difficult to see any significant difference in flower size when viewing the fully grown containers of Tulip 'Exotic Emperor'.

Images of just the flower heads highlight the fact that, while there might have been a small difference in the flower size, this difference was not significant.

The photo on the right shows a more mature flower; it is lighter white than the less mature buttery-coloured flowers on the left in the series of photos. It was noted that, even though the bulbs were planted at the same time and these photos are taken on the same day, the flowers from the larger bulb size appear to mature quicker.

Flaming Purissima

For the Flaming Purissima variety we found that the size of the flower produced was not dictated by the size of the bulb in our experiment, with the size difference being hardly distinguishable, as per the image of the flower heads on the slate. What was, however, noticeable was that the degree of maturity of the flower was opposite; the flowers produced by the smaller size bulbs reached maturity quicker than those produced by the superior size bulbs.

Unlike Exotic Emperor, which mature from a buttery to a white colour, Flaming Purissima mature

The flowers of Tulip 'Flaming Purissima', grown from three different bulb sizes, show little difference in final size.

The three different bulb sizes of Tulip 'Flaming Purissima' were all planted at the same time. The 9–10cm (3½–4in) bulb sized flowers in the left of the photo are more advanced compared to the larger bulb sized flowers in the right of the photo.

from very faint pink with a buttery middle on the outside of the petals, to a more intense pink, maintaining the buttery coloured central spine of the petal.

Conclusion

As growers, the results of our mini trial came as a surprise to us. It is possible that within different tulip types, the link between the size of the bulb and the size of the flower produced may yield different results. We would expect that for double or lily-flowering tulips results could be different, and this can undoubtedly become a recurrent task for ourselves and any keen grower who may want to explore links between growing material and results or performance.

TULIPS IN THE GARDEN

AFTER PLANTING CARE

Generally speaking, tulips are fairly trouble-free. Once planted in the ground it is largely a case of leaving them be through the winter and into the spring, allowing them to root and start to shoot. There are, however, a few things worth keeping an eye out for. One of the first vulnerabilities of freshly planted tulip bulbs often comes from pests. In the cold winter months, mice and squirrels can very easily get sustenance from bulbs that have not yet developed a root system and are therefore very easy pickings, with the only effort required being digging to lift the bulbs. Consequences of pest damage can often be devastating, especially within a commercial context. This is why securing mesh, chicken wire or other such aids in place straight after planting the bulbs and before them starting to root can be a wise first step in areas known to be prone to rodent pests. And while aesthetically it may not be an immediate improvement, it is a sacrifice worth making in the winter months.

Although not often a problem in the UK, equally important for countries where the autumn season may be dryer and warmer, is to monitor the moisture of the soil at the planting site. If necessary, it is important to ensure watering for the root system growth to be activated and enabled to establish. Ideally, the soil should

Wire mesh is placed temporarily over an area of freshly planted tulips to prevent squirrels digging the bulbs up. Once rooted and starting to shoot, squirrels are less likely to displace the bulbs and the wire can be removed.

stay damp but not waterlogged. The other factor worth monitoring at this point is weeding. With the general lack of vegetation, but the persistence and resilience of weeds, this is a good opportunity to ensure there are no weeds left so that, when the tulip bulbs start growing, there is no additional competition for light, moisture and nutrients from the soil. By the time spring arrives and the weather warms up, tulip bulbs should have developed a good fibrous root system that allows them to draw the volumes of water they require for their fleshy leaves and stems. Most tulip-growing locations have wet enough springs to provide enough water when they are grown in the ground. However, if the spring is particularly dry then some extra irrigation may be necessary. Feeding is helpful at this stage, but not as important as after flowering when the bulb is swelling in preparation for dormancy. A top dressing of an organic fertiliser such as bonemeal in the spring is a beneficial addition around the base of most bulbous plants, including tulips.

When tulips are in full leaf, they can use a large amount of water, particularly on a warm spring day. Extra irrigation may be necessary, especially in containers.

FLOWERING PERIOD

General information for flowering time is usually provided with the bulbs when purchased, with varieties usually categorised into three spring-flowering periods: early season, mid-season and late season. To be more specific with flowering time is very difficult as there are many factors that can affect the flowering time from year to year, with probably the most influential being the unpredictability of the weather. A cold spring could delay the flowering by two weeks, and conversely, a warm period in the spring can rapidly accelerate growth and result in flowering two weeks

Flowering time can vary significantly, depending on geographical location. Even within in a small flower bed, localised conditions can have a significant effect. In this case, the warmth retained by the surrounding walls has brought the closest plants into flower much earlier than those only three metres away.

An extreme example – here we see a red tulip in flower in a garden in Iceland. The photo was taken on 30 May, a good month later than we would expect to see this variety flowering in the UK.

Tulip 'The First' is often true to its name; it can be seen in flower as early as February, long before any other varieties are starting to show buds.

earlier than previous years. Commercially, much research has been conducted into flowering times under optimum temperatures, and guides are published for cut flower growers so that they can time their crop flowering to within days. Location is often an influencing factor alongside the weather; in more northern climes, the cooler winter and spring delays flowering time, whereas further south flowering occurs earlier. Within the UK the same variety grown in the north can flower up to two weeks later than in the south. Even within the north of England we have seen weeks of difference between tulips at the nursery in Preston on the warmer west coast and those grown at Constable Burton Hall in North Yorkshire, as mentioned in Chapter 7. The same is seen in the Netherlands where, with only 160km (100 miles) separating Lisse in the south of Holland and the northern province of Friesland, a flowering difference of up to three weeks can occur.

At the flowering extremes, early varieties can be seen flowering as early as February and late varieties as late as June. We have seen tulips in flower (albeit nearing the end of the flowering) as late as early July. That is far later than would be expected, indeed, and it is often a combination of factors involving a cold transition from spring into summer, combined with the location – a north-facing position that does not get

The tulips planted here are used as 'bedding' and will not be left in the ground once the display has finished, therefore there is no aftercare of the bulbs as fresh ones will be planted in the autumn to give as spectacular an effect the following year.

direct sunlight. Indeed, the planting aspect can influence significantly how far ahead or behind the flowering might be, as observed in some of the gardens we listed as destinations to see tulips. That being considered, in the UK, mid-April to the beginning of May tends to be a good time to see decent displays of tulips. A late planting will delay flowering to some extent, but plant too late and there is a chance that conditions are not cool enough for a long enough period for good root growth.

CARE AFTER FLOWERING

Tulips are often used as bedding plants, meaning that once the display has finished, the bulbs are taken out and replaced with other plants. When this is the case, there is no aftercare for the tulips. However, often when grown in containers, or when planted out somewhere where bulbs have established and come back every year, it is worth continuing to monitor and help bulbs along for the following year.

In commercial growing on the Dutch tulip fields, soon after flowering and before the formation of the seed pod, flower heads are cut mechanically en masse. While this may be seen as barbaric by those wanting to admire the beauty of the tulips, it is the best way for all the energy to be transferred from forming of the seed pod to bulking up of the bulb. On a small scale, when grown in gardens or in containers, this method of bolstering the size of the bulbs is not necessary, and the value of having blooms to admire for as long as possible outweighs the benefits of larger blooms.

The petals will be long gone by the stage of seed pod development, and with them, the reason for having tulips. However, this is an important stage in the life cycle of the plant as it is now that the tulip plant starts its preparation for dormancy and the

The act of flowering requires large amounts of energy to be expended. If the flowers are removed from the top of the stem just after formation, the nutrient is diverted to the bulb and larger bulbs are formed more quickly. Piles of tulip flowers are regularly seen at the side of Dutch fields.

Botanically, tulip seed pods are interesting to see developing, and it is interesting to observe how the shape of seed pods differs for different varieties.

It is important to note that some of the newer variegated varieties, such as *Tulipa praestans* 'Paradox', have very attractive foliage, even after the flowers have withered away.

Tulip 'Banja Luka'; a Darwin Hybrid. This group of tulips along with the Fosteriana group and species tulips are very good at naturalising.

following season's growing. If seedheads form, they should be removed unless you are aiming to collect the seed for sowing. Seed production is an extra drain on nutrient reserves and the removal of the seedhead after flowering allows all nutrients to be concentrated on bulb production. If the early summer is dry, watering may be required while the plants are still green. Feeding with either a top-dressing fertiliser such as bonemeal or a liquid fertiliser high in potassium when the flowers have finished will allow bulbs to replenish the energy they need to flower again the following spring.

While the foliage is still green, healthy and turgescent (end of April through to mid-May) tulips benefit from a final nutrient injection before going dormant for the summer. Once the foliage starts to wilt and become yellow, there is no need for feeding. It is important to replicate their natural habitat as much as possible during the dormancy period. On the slopes of the Tien Shan mountains where some tulips originate from, the bulbs will be baked in the sun throughout the summer and will benefit from significant levels of moisture during the autumn and winter seasons. For locations with a very variable summer such as the UK, which in the north can be generally much wetter than the mountain slopes of the tulips' origins, soil conditions play a major factor in summer dormancy and the actions a gardener has to take to ensure their tulips are in good health in the following year.

STORAGE OF THE BULBS

In the right conditions – that is, locations that stay very dry over summer, with light soils that are free draining as opposed to heavier soils that are prone to retaining dampness all summer long – bulbs will regrow and reflower regularly, especially those from certain tulip

Wire bottom Dutch crates are designed to allow a good flow of air to circulate around the tulip bulbs. They are also shallow so that heat cannot build up among the bulbs. Plastic crates are being used more and more now, due to their durability.

Tulips grow very well in pots, which offers great flexibility in moving them around. Tulip 'Flaming Flag', 'Candy Prince' and Tulip 'White Flag'.

groups including the Darwin Hybrid and species-type tulips. However, if these conditions cannot be supplied, bulbs can be harvested (dug up), dried out at the beginning of the summer and kept ideally in nets, which allow a continuous airflow during the storage period, or in paper bags, to prevent condensation, which could lead to the formation of mould on bulbs. It is important to avoid storing bulbs in containers made from plastic or other such materials that may not have breathability properties. Traditionally, the crates used in the Netherlands for storing bulbs lifted from tulip fields have a wire bottom to allow continuous airflow (often mechanically driven through the crates) during the storage period. The storage conditions must be dry and dark throughout the summer – a dry shed or a similar outbuilding (not damp and cool) would provide a good storage environment.

GROWING TULIPS IN CONTAINERS

Tulips in containers look fantastic anywhere in the garden in the spring and as displays are often changed yearly, container growing allows for experimenting with different varieties or colours. There are many other advantages or very good reasons for container growing. Lack of available ground space can be seen as a chief reason for those who want to enjoy the delights of tulip displays, but do not have the available ground space for planting in. A small backyard or frontyard can look equally uplifted by containers planted with colourful tulips. Similarly, people with limited mobility can still enjoy the process of planting and then watching tulips grow and bloom without needing to worry about digging or any other more involved form of soil preparation. The management of the process from planting to general caring is at a reduced scale, therefore much more accessible and more of an incentive to be involved with growing tulips.

Recent trends have also seen a significant increase in the use of more unconventional planting containers such as old tin baths, blue enamelware and repurposed objects with a vintage or antique look such as old milk and butter churns – something that seems to appeal to younger generations in particular. Not lastly,

Tulips can be grown in containers very successfully. Any container that holds the compost in place and allows water to drain away can be used. Here, an old tin bath (Tulip 'Candy Prince') and a wooden box (Tulip 'Van Eijk') are used to great effect.

This container is planted with Tulip 'Gold Fever' and *Muscari armeniacum* (Grape hyacinth); the contrasting yellow and blue work very well together.

as exemplified in Chapter 7, container tulip displays can look spectacular in themselves and achieve effects similar in impact to tulip-planted beds. Large, over-sized traditional terracotta containers offer endless possibilities of colour, shape and even species mixing – and help to create a mini-spring garden in a container.

How to plant in containers

When planting containers, you may choose to plant a single variety, or two, or more than two varieties. You can also intersperse other spring-flowering bulbs. Where more than one variety or species is planned for the same container, it is important when selecting combinations to ensure varieties will flower at the same, or very similar times, for the best displays. Good-quality soil-based or multipurpose potting composts available from garden centres and other horticultural suppliers are an excellent media for grow-ing tulip bulbs. When potting compost is used, it is important to monitor the watering once the tulips start growing. Soil-based composts have the advantage that they retain moisture better. Adding grit to enhance drainage can help in cases where heavier, soil-based composts are used. Always ensure that holes in the bottom of the containers allow the water to drain. The desired effect will dictate the bulb density to be planted; as a size guide, a 30cm × 30cm (12 × 12in) square container can be planted with sixteen tulip bulbs (four rows of four bulbs each) distributed equidistantly to achieve a full display.

In terms of aftercare, following flowering, we found that watering and feeding is more effective in containers, and storing the bulbs for the summer is also easier as they can be allowed to dry out by placing containers somewhere where they will not be watered, thus replicating the conditions in their natural habitat. Seedheads should also be removed as they are in a garden setting, for the reasons explained early in the chapter. Once bulbs from containers have been through their summer dormancy, they could be replanted into fresh compost in the same container or transferred into the garden allowing a different display to be created for the following year.

However, as it is often the case with plants and plant material, the requirements change radically with the season. Indeed, while it is important to allow tulip bulbs to dry out throughout the summer, insufficient watering when grown in containers is one of the main reasons why bud development fails. It is tempting to think we would offer tulip bulbs a boost to help them grow by placing containers in the greenhouse in the autumn. The likelihood is that bright autumn days translate into hot temperatures in greenhouses, which will be conducive to the compost drying out far more than can be tolerated by tulip bulbs. In addition, it is the cold weather that promotes rooting, and so depriving bulbs of cold weather will inhibit the rooting process significantly. All the above are good reasons as to why containers benefit from being placed straight outside after planting, or at the beginning of autumn if they are being reused after flowering the previous season. For bulbs kept in containers over summer, it is important to keep the compost dry to allow bulbs the dormancy period they need as part of their life cycle.

PERENNIALISATION

Customers and show visitors often talk about their struggles to get tulips to come back after a good flowering season. As detailed earlier in this chapter, replicating the natural habitat as closely as possible is

Tulipa saxatilis naturalised in a sunny woodland glade. Being perennial, they will appear each year in the spring.

the key to success for repeat flowering in the same spot. If the spot where tulips are planted is heavy clay, shaded and has long periods of being waterlogged while the bulbs are dormant and the root system is inactive, the likelihood is that bulbs will either rot before they restart to grow, or will be barely able to stay alive, and therefore not perform as well as they might. Conversely, if throughout the summer, after the plants have died down, they are allowed to stay very dry – if they are planted somewhere very sunny and they get 'baked' throughout the summer, the likelihood is that they will have spent their dormancy period in a healthy state and in autumn, when temperatures decrease and moisture from the rain becomes available, the root system will be ready to set off and the bud, already formed and sheltered by the scales within the bulb, will be ready to start growing. There is also a differentiation between the success rates of reflowering and different tulip types. Thus, Darwin Hybrids and Fosteriana types, are varieties more successful at reflowering than Double tulips and Parrot tulips. Even more so, species tulips which, similarly to Darwin Hybrids and Fosteriana types, have a single flower, are particularly good at being perennialised.

An interesting research study carried out in the United States has made a link between the success at perennialisation and the planting depth for bulbs. According to Miller (2019), a greater planting depth has resulted in increased rates of reflowering over a number of years. At our nursery in Preston, we decided to try out perennialisation for ourselves. We have created a raised bed and planted it with a wide range of tulip varieties, ensuring the planting depth of the bulbs was greater than 20cm (8in). Four years after planting,

Darwin Hybrid tulips in a raised bed on our nursery in Preston, Lancashire. Flowering just as well six years after planting.

it was noticeable that the varieties that have fared best are the Darwin Hybrids – specifically varieties such as Apeldoorn, Golden Apeldoorn, Banja Luka and Daydream.

PESTS AND DISEASES

There are a whole host of pests and diseases that affect tulips, from bacteria, fungi and viruses to aphids, slugs and squirrels. There has been extensive advice in the form of books written for commercial growers on tulip problems; however, on the whole, for the gardener there are only a handful of problems that are worth looking out for and controlling.

Rodents

In general, smaller scale cultivation, rodents such as mice and squirrels are the most often-encountered pests. It is difficult to underestimate their destructive potential. Both mice and squirrels are likely to dig the bulbs out soon after they have been planted in pots or in the ground, when the soil or compost is still soft, not yet having had the time to settle and compact around the bulbs. Also, the most vulnerable stage is before the rooting process has commenced, and there is no anchorage for the bulbs, meaning that they can be easily picked up and lifted by small, agile and enterprising rodents. The least visible damage tends to be the mark of little holes in pots or in the ground, or evidence that bulbs have been pulled out. The more obvious signs of a rodent attack include evidence such as partially eaten bulbs, roots or plant parts. Mice will nibble small holes into new shoots, seeking out the tasty bud towards the centre. This damage is often not noticed until the leaves develop fully. At the beginning of the chapter, we discussed the use of wire mesh as a covering to prevent physical removal of the bulbs and it is a worthy consideration for smaller scale planting in the ground or containers. This precaution works well against larger rodents such as squirrels and will deter mice, but mice are small and can squeeze past fine mesh.

There is some merit in planting plants or bulbs that act as deterrents. *Fritlllaria imperialis* (common name – Crown Imperial) has a pungent smell that mice and squirrels dislike. Similarly, some allium bulbs,

Mouse damage visible many weeks after it occurred when the new shoot that was just emerging was nibbled.

Evidence of rodent damage, mice will often nibble out the growing point of tulip bulbs, leaving behind 'bulb crumbs' as telltale signs even if the rest of the bulb has disappeared. They are very fond of species tulips often removing and relocating them.

Crown Imperials (*Fritillaria imperialis*) spot planted among tulips. The bulbs' pungent smell helps deter mice.

which smell of onions, have the same deterrent effect on rodents. While daffodil bulbs do not have a specific smell, they contain small quantities of toxins that are poisonous to rodents, and thus they afford some protection from grazing. All can be interplanted with tulips, creating a natural deterrent with the added benefit of increasing the diversity of species within a planting scheme. Pheasants, rabbits and deer will quite happily graze on tulip flowers and leaves and, apart from proofing gardens against these animals, it is difficult to offer much by way of prevention.

At our nursery in Preston, despite our efforts, every year we expect a small amount of loss through the activity of mice. For container growing, we find that elevating trays, pots, or containers on racking helps, as mice find it more difficult to climb. Danish trolleys, which are made of smooth metal, tend to be a sufficient deterrent.

Tulip fire

Botrytis tulipae is the fungus responsible for the most often-encountered disease affecting tulips – tulip fire. This is a disease specific to tulips, which manifests

Tulip fire is a fungal disease that appears as unsightly marking and distortion on the leaves and flowers. Often starting as a small blemish that quickly expands to larger brown patches, it looks very unattractive. Good garden hygiene and airflow is the best weapon against the fungus.

Tulip fire or frost damage?

Gardeners often question if damage to the leaves may be caused by tulip fire or by frost. In our experience, tulips have an exceptional tolerance to frost, and a remarkable ability to recover after frost. The bulbs themselves are very hardy and actually contain salts and sugars that effectively act as an antifreeze, stopping water crystals forming and rupturing the cells when conditions get very cold. Frost damage usually only occurs to freshly emerging shoots and, even then, more so to bulbs that have not been planted deep enough, 10cm (4in) or shallower. This is more often a problem in containers as there is less growing media to protect the bulbs. If a very cold spell is

itself by the appearance of distortions to the foliage, often accompanied by brown markings. Flowers affected by tulip fire present spots and markings and can have a shrivelled appearance. The texture of the petals is lacking the plumpness conferred by the water content.

The fungus is often harboured or spread in the ground, which is why container-grown tulips are largely shielded from this disease, if commercially available compost is used as the planting medium. Tulip plants affected by tulip fire should be pulled up as soon as possible and burnt, and not added to compost heaps, as this could allow the spread of the fungus around the garden. The advice given is to not use a planting location where the presence of tulip fire has been identified for three years. In our experience, it takes many more years to clear a site, and the surface spread can be surprisingly large. We have also noted anecdotally that some varieties are more susceptible to tulip fire, namely, dark or very dark-coloured varieties. There is no chemical control available to the amateur gardener.

As shoots emerge through the growing media or soil, they are at their most vulnerable to freezing conditions. Although we have had very few problems on our nursery in Preston, Lancashire, UK, if a prolonged severe cold spell is forecast it may be beneficial to temporarily cover the shoots with straw or horticultural fleece. This should be removed during the day if temperatures rise.

forecast when tulips are emerging, one step to take could be covering them with horticultural fleece or straw to provide some protection, but this must be removed as soon as possible so as not to create other problems. Having said all the above, we have grown tulips in quite small pots in north-west England for many years for our displays with very little damage from the cold.

If the markings are brown and spots are in the centre of leaves, the likelihood is that the plants are affected by tulip fire. If only the bottom leaves are affected by a whitening and thinning of the tissue – which can happen in containers or very dry areas – it is likely to be a result of the bulbs and compost or soil around them having dried out too much.

After three consecutive nights with heavy frost every morning, tulip displays at our nursery were down to the ground and looked irreversibly damaged. As soon as the sun came out and temperatures picked up slightly, the tulips in the display straightened up and returned to their expected appearance.

Aphids

While not considered a major pest of tulips, the presence of aphids can have a significant impact on the future health of tulip bulbs. Aphids will not do much physical damage unless it is a large infestation, but they are the main vector for the Tulip Breaking Virus or TBV, which we discuss next. In cooler climes they are not so much a problem and in the northern half of the UK tulips are rarely affected by aphids. If outbreaks do occur, especially during a warm spring or early summer, then some control will be necessary. Usually, a wash or spray down with soapy water is sufficient to rid the plants of a few aphids. If possible, it is important to avoid spraying chemicals as the wider impact on wildlife can be detrimental to the long-term control of such pests; insecticides could kill ladybird populations, which are a bio-control measure against aphids.

Tulip breaking virus (TBV), or tulip mosaic virus

There is some debate over which disease is more prevalent in tulips: tulip fire or TBV? Englemann and Hamacher (2008) argue that TBV is the most frequently encountered virus in the tulips. We are unsure if this may be geography specific, but in everyday nursery work, we have found TBV to be much rarer than tulip fire.

TBV is of extreme significance to the history of tulips and Tulipmania, as further explained in Chapter 10. The 'breaking' part of the TBV name refers to colour interruption that TBV induces, causing a feathery or stripy appearance, which is very striking and was much appreciated by tulip admirers throughout history. In 1928, Dorothy Cayley discovered the cause of the unusual pattern to be a virus. The virus is transmitted by aphids, and it has a weakening effect on bulbs and offshoots, which most tulip varieties do not survive long term. In the UK, the Wakefield and North of England Tulip Society (WNETS) maintains 'broken' tulip varieties (see Chapter 8 for further information).

We sometimes see very sporadic appearances of what might be a sign of TBV, manifested by the very occasional white line or similar discoloration. The exception where we have seen a clear effect of TBV has been Tulip Margarita. Tulip Margarita is a mauve double tulip, and the bulbs we grew exhibited creamy-yellow feathering patterns in the petals.

Tulip 'Margarita' showing no signs of TBV.

A flower of Tulip 'Margarita' showing mild effects of TBV.

Flower heads showing substantial effects of TBV.

Ilyonectria – A new tulip disease

In recent years there have been reports of a new disease affecting the foliage of Tulipa in Surrey, UK; namely, Ilyonectria sp. (2014). There have, however, not been any further documented reports of this disease having been identified elsewhere, evidence of further spread or further details of the impact of this disease on small or large-scale tulip cultivation in the UK.

Problems with flowering

While not a pest or disease, lack of flowering, referred to as 'growing blind', is a problem that gardeners experience. We are referring here to freshly planted bulbs expected to flower in the spring, and not to the problems associated with ground and climatic conditions causing smaller or no flowers in year two or three and onwards. Getting the best out of your tulips and perennialisation has already been discussed earlier in this chapter and the previous one. A fresh tulip bulb of the correct size is almost guaranteed to flower in the first year and blindness is almost always caused by growing conditions rather than the bulb being of poor quality. The most likely cause of a flower bud failing is that the bulbs have been kept too warm before planting or while growing. If bulbs are planted in borders outside it is unlikely that buds will fail because they will stay cool and well-watered but when planted in containers, it is important that they are still subjected to cool conditions for at least a few months. In a warm spring, containers of tulips will use a lot of water and they should not be allowed to dry out; otherwise buds will be at a greater risk of failing and therefore growing blind.

Drying out of containers because of insufficient water is one of the major causes of flower buds aborting.

CHAPTER 3 CASE STUDY

Tulip life cycle

Instead of a descriptive or narrative account, we felt it would be helpful to provide a visual account to the life cycle of the tulips to better explain the sequence of stages in the tulip's life cycle: emerging, flowering, wilting, then dormancy.

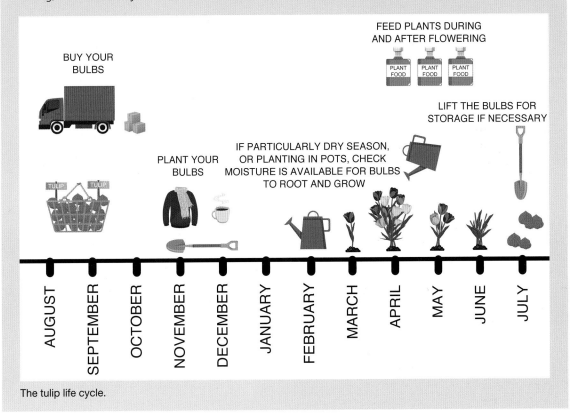

The tulip life cycle.

INCORPORATING TULIPS INTO YOUR GARDEN DESIGN

Garden design has a very important role in maximising the potential of spaces through landscaping and planting. We wrote this section with the assumption that readers expect advice on the bulb planting element of garden design, rather than more structural aspects related to hard landscaping creating lines and structures in the garden and space division. Our views given in this section are based on our experience of growing tulips, rather than experience in garden design, and for more complex design or re-design we believe that expert advice and the experience of a garden designer is always of value.

The analogy we would like to propose to our readers is to interior design. In the case of gardening, we suggest bulb planting should fulfil the equivalent role of 'finishing touches', in the way we might consider soft furnishing, wall art and other impermanent features and decorations. The hard landscaping and built elements of a garden are permanent, providing the constant structure. Likewise, trees, and especially mature trees, become permanent features of gardens. We would only move shrubs when they outgrow their location, or when they do not thrive where they have been planted – making them semi-permanent, somewhat similar to furniture in a dwelling. Bulbs, and especially spring-flowering bulbs, are the 'cushions' of the gardening world. Relatively inexpensive when compared to permanent and semi-permanent elements in the garden,

Tulip 'Ballerina' (underplanted with *Anemone blanda*) in a woodland coppice to give a burst of colour in the spring.

colourful bulbs in the spring can bring splashes of colour and excitement; they can be replaced or moved somewhere else with the same effect. The choice of colour is subjective, with no hard-and-fast rules when it comes to shape and colour, other than restrictions dictated by the growing environment.

We will make the assumption that when using ideas presented in this book and which are grounded in our tulip-growing experience, the levels and heights in gardens will already be in existence – provided by the presence of trees and shrubs and potentially herbaceous perennial plants, mindful at the same time that many of the herbaceous perennial plants have not quite got going for the growing season at the time when tulips are in flower. Having established this, it is safe to say that bulb planting allows for a lot more creativity and experimentation. As regards bulbs, there are somewhat fewer rules governing the appearance of a garden and more subjectivity is involved.

A final assumption we will make for this section is that the majority of readers will have an interest in how to include tulips in year-round gardens, therefore tulip bulbs will be planted among other existing annuals, herbaceous perennials, shrubs and trees in gardens. Not only is this a way to ensure continuous interest in the garden throughout the year, but it is also a realistic proposition of how to blend-plant in a way that will not draw attention to the different growth stages of the plants. As mentioned in Chapter 3, for some tulip varieties the foliage is attractive even after petals have disappeared. However, foliage that is withering is much better blended in among other plants in beds or borders, than it would be where no other plants may be present.

There are trends and new concepts often introduced by gardening celebrities on TV and radio gardening programmes that capture the public's imagination and make a specific plant or planting style particularly desirable. It is true to say that often our inspiration regarding planting schemes comes from places we have visited, and we have seen plant combinations that work incredibly well, that we might not necessarily have thought would work. The case study at the end of this chapter, as well as Chapter 7, provides our readers with ideas for destinations where they can see tulips in different settings, in gardens of different sizes – and be inspired or get new ideas of how they may plant tulips in their own gardens.

Tulips play an important role in garden design, as they are the only species to provide such an extensive

Tulips are one of the few genera that cover almost every colour in the spectrum, with the only missing colour being a true blue. Many varieties have been named with blue in the title like this double tulip 'Blue Diamond', but it is clearly not blue, but more of a purple colour.

colour range at a time of the year when there is relatively little colour in the garden. They are a preamble to the joy and excitement provided by our gardens for the rest of the year, therefore a much-used plant in early displays in private and public gardens and spaces across the world.

COLOUR SCHEMES

Monochromatic planting

Subjectivity is a good point to start this particular section with, as gardens are first and foremost private spaces meant to reflect our personal views of what is important, and our preferences for perhaps including

A pink general overview with a rich texture given by other plant species is good example of monochromatic planting.

fantastic contributors to single-colour borders or themed beds, adding height and structure at a time of the year when most perennial plants have not yet gained a lot of height, and most spring-flowering bulbs are generally not very tall.

For many years now, customers have told us of their preference for single- or predominant-colour gardens. White gardens, or white cottage gardens tend to be in the top preferences. White gardens are sometimes referred to as 'moon gardens'. A moon garden will have a specific focus on white flowers, silver foliage or variegated plants that reflect the light of the moon in the dark, and plants with scented flowers that open at night. Moon gardens with this remit have found more popularity in the US. In the UK, there is an increasingly growing interest in moon gardens, but more with the aim of providing a good environment for night pollinators. Taking this planting style as an example, depending

Tulip 'Queen of Night' is an extremely popular variety, more a very dark purple than pure black. It works well for gardeners who wants a dark-themed border or garden.

or excluding certain colours, plants or certain types of plants. And for every one individual who dislikes the smell of lilies (*Lilium regale*), the likelihood is that there are at least five individuals who adore that scent. The same applies in the case of preferences for colours, shapes and different types of plants.

When we talk about monochromatic gardens, we refer to the overall impression in terms of colour given by a collection of plants, rather than an expectation that all plants included in the planting scheme would be that exact colour. Thus, plant variations such as complementary, slightly lighter or slightly darker colours, viridiflora features (green colour present in the petals), slight flushing on the outside of the petals can be included with confidence in a monochrome planting scheme, as it will provide a much richer texture, more interest and diversity. Tulips lend themselves well to monochromatic gardens; in spring, tulips are on the aspect, the levels of light, the type of soil and the space available, other plants that tulips could be combined with, or perennials that may come into flower as the tulips fade away are listed in Table 4.1.

Similarly to the white gardens, the black, or very dark gardens are equally popular with gardeners. We often encounter the constant fascination with black flowers, Tulip 'Queen of Night' remaining one of the most popular tulip varieties. This is closely followed by blue gardens, where the pervasive colour scheme is blue, although it may allow for complementary lighter colours that may accent or emphasise the intensity of the blue. Similarly popular are the hot gardens, where the planting schemes favour colours resembling heat or fire, and where orange, yellow and red plants take centre stage.

Subjectivity is the common denominator here, with gardeners choosing to surround themselves with their preferred colour and leave the leeway and nature's input to play their role through the changing textures given by different types of plants, foliage, growth habits, shape and structure.

Examples of white tulip varieties currently commercially available that can be added in combinations with the plants listed in Table 4.1 include varieties such as:

- Tulip Hakuun
- Tulip White Triumphator
- Tulip Agrass White
- Tulip White Flag

Tulip 'Yokohama' and Tulip 'Princess Irene' lend themselves to being used in hot-themed gardens.

Table 4.1 Good plant pairings for tulip in white planting schemes

White gardens				
Spring-flowering bulbs	**Ground cover**	**Herbaceous perennials**	**Shrubs**	**Trees**
Narcissus 'Thalia'	Pachysandra terminalis 'Variegata'	Lychnis coronaria 'Alba'	Weigela 'White Lightning'	Eucalyptus gunnii
Narcissus 'Paper White'	Vinca minor alba 'Variegata'	Brunnera macrophylla 'Jack Frost'	Euonymus fortunei 'Emerald Gaiety'	Betula utilis 'Jacquemontii'
Narcissus 'Mount Hood'	Claytonia sibirica	Senecio cineraria	Hebe albicans	Fagus sylvatica
Narcissus poeticus 'Pheasant's Eye'	Myosotis 'Alpestris White'	Pulmonaria 'Sissinghurst White'	Hebe 'White Wand'	Acer capillipes
Narcissus 'Pueblo'		Euphorbia characias 'Silver Swan'	Potentilla 'Abbotswood'	
Allium 'Graceful Beauty'			Azalea 'Geisha White'	
Allium karataviense			Cornus alba 'Elegantissima'	
Anemone nemorosa			Ilex aquifolium 'Silver Queen'	
Muscari 'White Magic'				

Tulip 'Purissima', Tulip 'Spring Green' and Tulip 'White Rebel' are all white tulips that combine with plants in Table 4.1 to create a monochromatic design.

- Tulip Royal Virgin
- Tulip Swan Wings
- Tulip Purissima
- Tulip White Dream
- Tulip White Rebel
- Tulip Mondial
- Tulip Spring Green
- Tulip Sapporo.

This is not an exhaustive list, with many more other varieties being bred and made available.

Regardless of colour combinations chosen, depending on the effect desired and the space available, tulips can be used to add structure when combined with plants with a different growth habit. In terms of visual impact, however, gardeners may choose to avoid planting tulips in a solitary fashion, or very few bulbs with an excessive distance between them.

Bi-colour (two-colour) colour schemes

Moving through the colour palette, the obvious progression from monochrome gardens is the bi-colour garden, border or planting scheme. Here, we are not talking about bi-colour plants, such as Tulip Monsella Monsella; we are referring to a combination of two

When referring to bi-coloured schemes, we mean two different-coloured plants rather than two colours on one flower. Tulip 'Monsella' is an example of the latter.

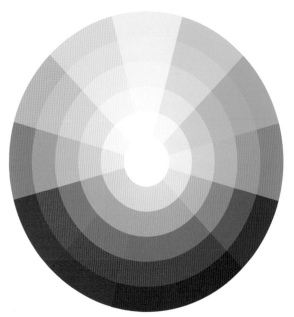

The colour wheel is a good starting point to decide on the colour combination desired.

A bi-coloured planting scheme using Tulip 'White Triumphator' and Tulip 'Queen of Night'. The white and black colours contrast with each other very well, allowing each of them to shine.

different varieties, or even two completely different plant species, which has been decided upon with colour in mind as the main reason for association.

A very useful tool when deciding on colour combinations can be a colour wheel, alongside considering some principles of colour theory. Firstly, the three primary colours – red, yellow and blue – are so called as they cannot be obtained by mixing other colours. Secondary colours are orange, purple and green, so called because they have been obtained by mixing two of the primary colours. Finally, the six tertiary colours, which are magenta, vermilion, violet, teal, amber and chartreuse. Including shades and tints will darken and lighten colours respectively and create much more than twelve colour combinations. A colour wheel has the colour groups clustered together and

helps visualise potential combinations. When talking about colour palettes, there are three types of palettes that are relevant. A monochromatic palette or colour scheme is obtained by using shades of a single colour. Earlier in this chapter, the example of moon gardens was given, where the prevalent colour for flowers is white, but different plant species might bring different shades and tones of white to the mix, with silver foliage also contributing to the overall colour. The second type of colour palette is the analogous palette, where two or three colours that sit next to each other on the colour wheel are used, usually thus avoiding colour contrasts. Finally, complementary palettes are those formed by using colours that sit opposite one another on the colour wheel, thus creating contrasting colour combinations.

The other aspect to be mindful of when it comes to colour combinations in the garden is visual harmony. In the case of colours, harmony refers to colour combinations that are pleasing visually – not so static and predictable that the combination may be considered dull, but at the same, time not so thought-provoking that they become a challenge or a puzzle to resolve. In the context of plants and planting schemes, colour is not the only factor to predict visual harmony. Texture as well as colour can contribute to the balance of visual

Tulip 'Queensland' and *Muscari* 'Alaska', a good example of texture alongside colour, resulting in a harmonic ensemble.

A contrasting colour combination between species could be *Muscari armeniacum* with yellow Tulip 'Monte Carlo' – a combination famous for Keukenhof Gardens, or *Muscari* 'Album' with black tulips.

harmony. It is also worth returning to the point of subjectivity and reiterating that boundaries and limits for what may be deemed harmonious or disharmonious in terms of colour combinations can be very individual and dictated by context and background, and so relying on one recipe alone for what might constitute harmony would be a brave undertaking. A final thought to consider when thinking about colour schemes and colour combinations is the context in which this applies. Within gardening so much that is linked to plant colour is also impacted by other factors such as light, temperature and humidity. Growing tulips for many years has been a good way to learn that colour can change substantially from the younger stages of the plants to the mature stage. While applying colour principles will always be a matter of personal choice for gardeners, being aware of them can help with the planning and selecting of plants.

An analogous combination of Tulip 'Black Parrot' and 'Blue Diamond'.

Bi-colour combinations can be based on contrasting colours, such as black or very dark purple with white or yellow. In this type of combination, the contrast allows both varieties to stand out, with the vibrancy of the brighter colour being punctuated by the dark colour.

The colours used in a bi-colour mix can also be analogous. Analogous colours are those that are close to each other on the colour wheel. Examples of such colour combinations include lilac and purple combinations, pink and burgundy, or orange and red.

Neutral colour schemes

Finally, neutral colours can have a tremendous impact in colour schemes. Neutral colours will not necessarily alter significantly the impact of colour combinations, but they might enhance it, or tone it down. In gardening, neutral colours are mainly white, cream, silver and green. In some instances, glaucous colours (bluish-grey or bluish-white) can act as neutral colours when used similarly to silver foliage.

In the context of gardening, green is the ubiquitous, staple garden colour, and therefore an unquestionably neutral colour that will support and enhance a colour mix, be it with analogous or contrasting colours. Similarly, including cream into colour schemes often has the effect of enriching texture in overall appearance. Tulips are all about different colours and some gardeners may find guidance for colour combinations useful, especially gardeners who may take a systematic approach to choosing colours they might like in their gardens. Nevertheless, experimenting with colour and taking the approach of colour explosions can give spectacular results in the right circumstances, often related to the space available and the context.

PLANTING DENSITIES

In Chapter 2 we provided information on planting densities in terms of cultivation notes. In this section we consider planting densities in relation to garden design as opposed to cultivation notes. By that, we mean that we will look at the conditions in which tulips thrive, but also achieve a visual impact appropriate for the reasons or the context for which tulips have been planted.

There are several factors to be taken into consideration when thinking of planting density. Firstly – what is the aim of the display? Is it for a commercial purpose, to showcase a specific variety? Is there interest in the foliage? What is the growth habit – is it a single headed type or a multi-headed type of tulip? Is it for containers, for a backyard where everything is grown in containers, or for a small garden with existing planting in situ? Is the planting scheme for a public space or a park, where there is ample space available? Attention should also be paid to the size and shape of the blooms when reaching maturity. For example, in the case of multi-headed tulips planted in a location where space availability is not a concern, the planting density for bulbs can be 15–18cm (6–7in) apart. When flowers reach maturity and blooms open, this density will allow for a display where plants and flowerheads can be seen easily. For a large planter with a 60cm (24in)

diameter we have used approximately fifty bulbs to produce an impactful display.

Oversized terracotta planters are an excellent way to display tulips combined with other spring bulbs. The successful approach is to ensure that the compost is not visible. In the photograph below, this was achieved by including in the planting *Myosotis* (Forget-me-not), which here plays the role of ground cover.

Concepts introduced by garden designers may not always be easily transposed in smaller gardens, but the principles behind planting schemes can still be applied on a smaller scale. World-renowned garden designer Piet Oudolf has introduced the concept of fuzzy drift planting. This is applicable to larger spaces and the public realm, and it is well suited to taller growing herbaceous perennials, but it has been applied to early

Multi-headed tulip varieties planted further apart can give the same effect as singles planted closer, therefore saving on the number of bulbs required. *Tulipa praestans* 'Paradox'.

Oversized terracotta planters are an excellent way to display tulips combined with other spring bulbs. The successful approach is to ensure that the compost is not visible.

spring bulbs also with great success, exemplifying an impression of bulb naturalisation with the use of botanical species *Tulipa clusiana* 'Lady Jane' mixed among *Narcissus* 'Thalia' and planted so that it gives the impression of drifts.

In his designs, and through his choice of variety, Oudolf retains an appearance close to what it might be in the natural habitat. The very dainty *clusiana* tulip is representative of other botanical species with the much finer leaves. It gives the impression of a delicate plant that would respond to the elements and sway with the breeze. The red flushing on the outside of the petals disappears to reveal a very delicate-looking, entirely white centre. In reality, botanical tulips are among the best species at naturalising and reflowering in the right conditions.

Dutch garden designer Jacqueline van der Kloet takes the concept of drift planting and applies it to the more intensely coloured tulip hybrids with excellent results for private gardens and public spaces.

APPROPRIATE TYPES OF TULIPS FOR DIFFERENT SETTINGS

In our experience, the main pull factor as far as tulips are concerned is colour. As explained previously, colour is a stimulus of often underestimated potency and usually the first attribute of tulips to attract attention. It is, however, important whenever possible to consider other attributes of the varieties and their suitability to the planting location. One of the most frequent questions we are asked is about the hardiness of tulips. They may have a delicate appearance, but in our experience, tulips are remarkably hardy, with an astounding ability to shake off the frost and revert to a standing position even when they have been affected by frost during the night. Although not often, we have seen at our nursery swathes of tulips flattened to the ground after a night's heavy frost which, before midday, have recovered to the extent that they looked like they had never experienced any such weather incident.

Related to weather and location specificity, people who have gardens that are more exposed to windy conditions request varieties that are shorter, with sturdier stems. Short tulip varieties from the Kaufmanniana and Greigii groups have long been favoured for rockeries, low containers and for growing conditions where a short, sturdy stem help ensure the display will last for as long as possible. Several Kaufmanniana varieties have been suggested in Chapters 1 and 6.

As well as the shortest varieties, the Triumph group includes medium height tulips (approximately 40cm/16in stem length), which offer a bigger breadth of shape and colour and, in some locations, might fulfil

Botanical tulips planted in a drift have gained more currency in garden design, following designer Piet Oudolf starting the drift trend.

These photographs of tulips affected by frost were taken shortly after 7am, at which point they looked irretrievable; Tulip 'Doll's Minuet' (left), Tulip 'Quebec' (right).

The same tulips photographed later the same day, shortly after 4pm looking perfect and showing that tulips are quite resilient and hardy; Tulip 'Doll's Minuet' (left), Tulip 'Quebec' (right).

Tulip 'Pinocchio' has always been one of our favourites for short, sturdy varieties. Height: 25cm (10in).

the requirements for height and withstand weather conditions. There are many varieties that have long been favoured by the public from the Triumph group. We would like to single out the Prince range (Candy Prince, Purple Prince, Sunny Prince), which are part of this group and which, in addition to the medium length stem, have a oblong-shaped flower head; this maintains a closed appearance through to maturity and even after. This is preferred by some gardeners as, without the regular reopening of the petals due to light intensity, flowers continue to look fresh throughout the growing season.

The opposite in terms of height can also be the case. When considering planting so as to achieve an early spring wildflower meadow effect, taller tulip varieties might be sought to complement other plants included in the planting scheme, such as tall daffodils. Of course, an authentic look will be given by the right mix and diversity of species included – thus, not every species in this planting style needs to be the same height. An excellent example is the springtime beds under the pleached lime trees from Gresgarth Hall Gardens, planted with a variety of spring-flowering plants, bulbs, and Tulip Queen of Night.

Tulip 'Candy Prince', 'Purple Prince' and 'Sunny Prince' (left to right) are all from the 'Prince' range of tulips. This range grows to 35cm (14in) with a sturdy stem and flowers that retain their shape throughout flowering.

For the medium-height tulips with vibrant colours, we would also recommend Tulip 'Jimmy' (Triumph, 40cm/16in), Tulip 'Hotpants' (Triumph, 50cm/20in) and Tulip 'Caractere' (Triumph, 50cm/20in) (left to right).

GROWING TULIPS IN THE GARDEN FOR CUT FLOWERS

Our nursery space in Preston allows us the flexibility to install tulip cutting beds. In 2020 when, due to having Covid-19 restrictions in place, we were unable to hold our yearly Tulip Open Weekend event, no one was able to see the thousands of tulips we had planted before the pandemic began. The cutting beds, however, meant that we could leave bunches of tulips at the gate for passers-by to help themselves, and so, indirectly, the cutting beds became the only part of the nursery seen by the public that year.

Tulips as cut flowers look equally impressive when they adorn the interior of the home. In our experience, many of the double-flowered varieties that reach a height of over 40–50cm (16–20in) struggle to sustain the weight of the flower head and are liable to collapse in a planted bed. Often those will be the first tulips we use as cut flowers.

Traditionally, for cut flowers we bear in mind specifically the length of the stem. While that is relevant when the vase or container we plan to use may be designed for longer stems, that is not always absolutely necessary for tulips. Tulips are the only cut flower where the stem continues to elongate after it has been cut. To illustrate this, we have included here photographs of Tulip Kansas Proud, which shows stem elongation of around 10cm (4in) over a five-day period.

The case study for this chapter is a great illustration of tulip planting that brings back colour in spring, in a private garden in the northwest. However, the main points we hope that this chapter has highlighted is that, in our view, tulip planting in the garden needs firstly to

Tulips grown in the garden can look equally spectacular when cut and displayed in a vase, particularly double long-stemmed tulips that can be prone to falling over in inclement weather. Tulip 'Finola' (pink) and Tulip 'Margarita'.

Tulip 'Kansas Proud' was cut at our nursery and placed in a vase on 10 May (left); 12 May (middle) and 15 May (right) are of the same vase. This shows not only that the flowers have opened, but also that the stems have elongated: tulips are one of the very few cut flowers that continue growing after cutting.

respond to the needs of those using the gardens, and subjectivity in the choice of colours, variety and planting scheme is welcome and should be encouraged. Secondly, it is good to get inspiration from places we visit that display tulips exceptionally well. And thirdly, related to the second point, when we are not quite ready or confident enough to experiment with colours or varieties we like, it is good to attempt a planting scheme seen elsewhere. Not all tulip combinations are successful for several reasons, and eliminating the testing stage can save time, money, and a season's worth of an unsatisfactory display.

CHAPTER 4 CASE STUDY

Growing tulips in a northwest garden

Jack Green Cottage, Preston, Lancashire

Nestled in Brindle, in the heart of Lancashire, Jack Green Cottage oozes charm and authenticity. The property is surrounded by one acre of thoughtfully crafted mature gardens. The sweeping drive from the gate to the cottage allows the wanderer to explore and imagine what surprises and hidden gems might be found in the different parts of the garden. Spring is a particularly exciting time at Jack Green Cottage, with unexpected and joyful garden encounters in all the different parts of the garden. We have selected Jack Green Cottage garden for the different ways in which the owners make tulip displays look and feel very much at home within the established garden.

In the year of writing of this book, at the front of the cottage, a bold display of red and white tulips brought to life a shrub- and topiary-dominated border of a large grassed area. Indeed, although sunny days are all that is needed to bring gardens to life in spring, it is easy to see how much more of an uplift the

A mix of red and white tulips planted in a part of the garden viewable from the windows of Jack Green Cottage.

This good example of a sharply contrasting bi-colour planting scheme used in this part of the garden is a bold statement, in tune with the formality of the topiary trees surrounding the tulip planting.

colour combination used in this planting scheme brings. The varieties used here – Agrass White, Pieter De Leur and Apeldoorn – maintain a degree of formality suitable to accompany the existing topiary structure using the bi-colour planting scheme, as described in more detail earlier in this chapter. At the same time, however, it brightens up and creates a point of focus for a part of the garden that might otherwise be overlooked.

To the right-hand side of the cottage, there is a well-established perennial long border which, in spring, offers clusters of colour, shape and texture dotted through existing planting emerging after winter.

Natural shelter offered by the external stone gable end of the cottage and a two-foot (half-metre) elevation created with the help of a natural stone wall, make excellent use of the multilevel nature of the space. The wall creates an ideal space for growing tulips, benefitting from the shelter at the gable end, as well as the enhanced drainage, which is often a requirement for growing tulips and other spring-flowering bulbs successfully.

The approach to planting tulips in this perennial border – where softer colour combinations are mixed in an analogous fashion – is a sharp contrast to the bi-colour planting scheme near the topiary

Clumps of tulips are planted through this well-established, long herbaceous border to create extra spring interest before the other perennial planting reaches maturity in the summer. Tulip 'Quebec' (centre front), Tulip 'Synaeda Blue' (centre back).

area. Indeed, the softer colour palette complements the organic return to life movement in the perennial border, whereas the sharp red and white contrast is well-balanced by the clear lines of the topiary and the hedge surrounding it. Making the most of the existing shrubs, for instance, the purple *Berberis thunbergii* 'Atropurpurea' make the colour scheme well balanced and pleasing to the eye.

At the back of the cottage, more elevated retaining natural stone walls, combined with a southwesterly position, provide further scope for tulips to thrive in the spring sun. Steps up from the back door and onto the terrace divide the space neatly between a perennial border and a herb garden during the summer. In spring, however, tulips are allowed to spring up in both the decorative half and the utilitarian half of the terrace. The addition of garden art visible through colourful bare branches in the spring in the form of fairy tale statues complements gardening skills and taste, with character sculptures that suggest a magic place and the perfect harmony of the place they inhabit.

The expansive grassed space leading onto the Victorian glasshouse allows for spring-flowering

Tulip 'Daydream' (orange) has naturalised well in the sunny open borders toward the top of the gardens at Jack Green Cottage.

bulbs, mature trees, hedging and spotting shrubs to co-exist in perfect harmony and in a shire-like setting. As described throughout this chapter, the garden surrounding Jack Green Cottage is a good example of tulip bulbs planted to act as colourful addendums to existing structures, giving gardeners the flexibility to change their mind, move patches of colour if they so wish, or add to them, in order to welcome the new growing season, without affecting the overall structure of the garden.

Jack Green Cottage gardens present a beautiful illustration of how tulip planting does not need to be formal in order to lift, illuminate and bring energy to environments dominated by vast expanses of grass, mature trees and uneven landscape. Similarly, the gardens at Jack Green Cottage show how working with the existing features as a canvas offers the possibility to change displays with spectacular results.

Jack Green Cottage is a private garden open to the public as part of the National Garden Scheme.

As discussed earlier in this chapter, the tulips planted in this garden show how they can be used to enhance the existing structure, and features within the garden.

PROPAGATION AND BREEDING

A tulip is a perennial herbaceous plant, meaning that it comes back each year and grows fresh leaves, stems and flowers. In the case of a tulip, this happens because the bulb that forms underground acts as storage vessel for all parts of the plant and nutrients to fuel that regrowth in the subsequent year. We can use this to our advantage when it comes to propagation. The main dif-ference between a bulb and a seed is that the seed contains the genetic coding to allow a new plant to grow, rather than having all the parts of the plant already formed, as in the case of a bulb. However, the seed allows for breeding new varieties because the genetic coding changes when different varieties are cross-pollinated.

Seeds and bulbs offer gardeners two different ways to propagate tulips with differing results. Seeds will potentially grow new varieties but take many years to develop into flowering plants. Bulbs contain an exact copy of the tulip plant they came from and will flower the year after we plant them, if they are sufficiently big.

MULTIPLICATION OF BULBS

Most bulbs will readily produce offsets, and tulips are no different. Offsets are small bulbs, often called bulblets, that develop from a bud above the basal plate at the base of the mother bulb. The bulblets are fed from the mother bulb and can affect the performance of the mother bulb due to the nutrient drain. Alongside the other reasons discussed in Chapter 2 regarding the lifting of tulip bulbs, lifting in the summer allows these bulblets to be removed from the mother bulb. In Chapter 9 we look at how this happens on a com-mercial scale.

Bulblets

Bulblets are exact copies of the mother bulb and they will perform in just the same way as the parent bulb

The smaller offsets will not flower until they are bigger bulbs. They could take three or four years of growing on until flowering size is reached. The tulips pictured here are in their third year of growing and will probably flower in the following year.

A tulip bulb with its offsets or bulblets still attached after harvesting, cleaning and drying. The offsets can now be removed, with the smaller ones immediately replanted to stop drying out and the larger ones stored until the autumn for planting.

including flower height, colour and form. Multiplication using the new bulblets is a form of vegetative propagation that can be taken advantage of to produce new flowering bulbs. The mother bulb under natural growing conditions usually produces four or five bulblets measuring 5–10mm (¼–½in) across. Some varieties will produce very few bulblets, while others produce many more, which can be commercially advantageous, allowing stocks of bulbs to be multiplied quicker. The small bulblets are usually removed from the mother bulb after lifting in the summer and are potted up straight away into good-quality, free-draining compost so they don't dry out.

They could be planted straight out into the garden, but they are quite vulnerable to pests, particularly mice and squirrels, who will treat them like a quick tasty snack. When small, the bulblets are also prone to drying out, so the pots should be kept slightly damp for the summer, but certainly not wet or water-logged. The bulblets are unlikely to flower in the following spring, but by the summer they should have increased in size to a point where they can be treated in the same way as a larger bulb. It will usually take three to four years for a bulblet to reach flowering size.

Micropropagation

Micropropagation, also known as tissue culture, is a laboratory-based technique of creating new plants from a very small amount of existing plant material. The process is a scientific one, conducted in super sterile conditions in a lab, with all factors from nutrients to water strictly controlled. A small section, measuring only a few millimetres, of tulip growing tip is cut from a bulb. This tissue is placed into a test tube containing a gel-like substance called a culture, which contains all the necessary nutrients and creates the perfect conditions for rapid cell division to occur within a matter of weeks. The mass of cells that grows is then sliced up and transferred to a different culture that promotes shoot and root growth and, in the case of tulips, the formation of miniature bulbs. In a matter of a few weeks, thousands of new bulblets can be created, and these will then be grown on in a soil-based system. This type of propagation also enables previously virus-infected stock to be 'cleaned'. The virus in a bulb takes time to catch up with the growth of the tulip, so the growing tip is effectively always virus free. Because just the growing tip of the tulip is taken in this method, the virus is not transferred. Micropropagation is in its infancy for tulip production and research is ongoing, but results appear promising.

An extract from an article on the Hortipoint website highlights the importance of micropropagation:

'Hans van den Heuvel, Managing Director R&D Dümmen Orange: "Now that the breeding process of tulips from the moment of crossing to the delivery of a commercial bag of bulbs no longer lasts 20 years, but only 6–7, we'll be able to respond more effectively to the changing demand of consumers and the market, just like for other ornamental plants. We'll also be able to test seedlings faster on resistance and their cultivation and forcing qualities. The technique fits in well with our innovation plans for tulip. In September, we'll use a number of varieties to test flowering induction in tulips and very early stage screening for diseases such as TVX, fusarium and TBV." '

For some tulip varieties that are very slow to multiply, micropropagation could be a quicker way of producing stocks of tulip bulbs than the traditional method of bulb division. It is still in its infancy as a new technique. Tulip 'Tom Pouce'.

PROPAGATION FROM SEED

Tulips will grow from seed but aside from tulip breeders, it is unlikely gardeners would consider growing tulips from seeds, let alone try it. That is because propagation from seed is a time-consuming process that can have very variable results and most gardeners when planting a certain plant, in this case tulips, are doing so because they want a certain colour, shape or height flower or they wish to create a certain effect, as we can see in the design chapter. Having said this, multiplication of some tulip species can be very successful from seeds. We often get asked about growing from seed and there is scant information available in general tulip texts; including details here will hopefully help some gardeners. Even if growing tulips from seed is not a plan, we think it is useful to know about what it involves, for greater understanding of the tulip and its life cycle.

Pollination

Pollination occurs when pollen from one of the six anthers transfers to the central triangular stamen. Tulip flowers grown outside can be pollinated by bees, insects, wind and animals. Being self-fertile they will also self-pollinate, so even in isolation they can

Tulip seed pods come in various lengths and girths. Most hybrids form triangular-shaped pods.

The stigma of this tulip flower has been fertilised and has started to swell, while the anthers and petals have shrivelled but have not yet dropped off.

Tulips are self-fertile and can be pollinated by the wind and various insects including bees, as seen here on *Tulipa turkestanica*.

produce seed. A lot of hybrids, however, do not pollinate easily due to complicated genetics, making them sterile.

Seed development

If a tulip stamen is successfully fertilised, seed production will follow on from flowering. The tulip drops its petals and the stamen at the centre of the flower will swell and elongate as the embryos form. This usually occurs over a four-week period. The seed then needs to mature in the pods. Once the seed pod is fully formed, the leaves start to turn from green to a light brown followed by the stem, with the seedhead usually being the last part to change colour. While green, the pod will remain tightly closed as the seed development or 'ripening' continues inside, sheltered from the worst influences of the weather, be that cold, wet or even heat. Tulip seed pods are generally an elongated, triangular shape. The seeds vary between species and hybrids but are usually thin (2–3mm/1/16–1/8in thick), papery and roughly round.

Seed collection and preparation

Seeds usually reach maturity twelve weeks after pollination. The seed pods can be left to dry naturally on the plant, but it is often better to remove them from the plant before they have split open and are still turning from green to brown. Pods left in situ often fall to the ground before they are dry, get eaten or, depending on the climate, end up staying too wet and rot before they can be collected. The seeds are very light and papery and the wind can easily blow them away once the pods split. The seed pod can be removed from the plant while it is still green, but ideally has started to dry slightly. As long as the rest of the plant has browned off, pods should be ready to be removed. Most likely this will be well into the summertime, around June or July in the UK. Pods like these should be placed in trays, in a warm, dry location out of direct sunlight to finish the drying process. As the pods dry and change colour, they will eventually split and by this time the seed inside will also have dried and changed colour from green to anywhere from almost transparent to light brown to dark brown. The transparent seeds should be discarded as they will not be viable, but the dark seeds will have a bit more weight to them due to the formed embryo. These are the seeds we need to collect for planting. Saved seeds are best sown in the same year of collecting, as viability deteriorates quickly in storage.

Tulip seeds are fine and papery and can very easily be damaged or lost, so care should be taken to store them somewhere dry until planting in the autumn. Saved seeds do not store well and should be sown the same year as harvesting.

Seed pods, that have been collected to stop them getting too wet, are laid out to dry in trays, which will catch the seeds as the pods open.

SEED SOWING

Seeds should be sown late summer or early autumn as they need a winter chill, known as stratification, followed by a warmer period to stimulate growth. Seeds could in theory be sown straight into a flower border and left to it; this after all is what happens in the wild. However, after going to all the effort of collecting, drying and grading the seed, it is better to give it the best chance of germination and subsequent survival by growing in containers or dedicated, specially prepared beds.

By far the easiest way to grow from seed is in containers; it is easier to maintain ideal growing conditions for the small bulbs that develop in the first couple of years and to protect them from pests and predators.

To prevent seedlings getting lost in the garden and to provide protection from predators, seeds are best sown in pots. A cold frame or cool greenhouse is very useful for winter protection for the very delicate seedlings.

A large-scale propagation bed in the Netherlands. Seeds and young bulblets are grown in trays to facilitate harvesting, and fleece pulled over small hoops protects the seedlings from the worst of the weather while growing.

The freshly sown seeds are covered with a layer of compost and then fine sand. The weight of the sand stops seeds being pushed beyond the growing surface. If not enough sand is used, the seeds become exposed and can be damaged by the weather.

These containers could be terracotta or plastic, but deep rather than shallow pots are best, as this will give the developing tulip bulb plenty of growing media to develop in. A good-quality multipurpose compost mixed with grit or sand to improve drainage is ideal. Fill a pot three-quarters full and lightly firm the surface; seeds should be placed onto the surface so that they do not overlap, but they can be sown almost touching. The seeds should be covered with half a centimetre (¼in) of sieved compost and then a thin layer of grit or sand. Water well, ideally in a tray of rainwater to allow the compost to absorb the moisture. The seeds now need a cold spell, so they are best left outside or, if available, in a cold frame. The seeds will germinate when the temperatures start to rise in the spring and, initially, the seedling will look very much like grass. It is best not to prick them out at this stage, as they will not have developed a bulb yet and are unlikely to survive being moved. Once the seeds have germinated, the pots can be placed under cover if not in a cold frame, to give the new seedlings some protection from any poor spring weather. The seedlings are quite fragile at this stage and should not be allowed to dry out or to overheat, so some protection from direct sun may be needed, particularly in the first few growing seasons.

Bulb development following germination

The seedlings will start to develop bulbs in the first year of growth, but they will be too small to transplant

Seedlings at various stage of growth (left to right): two- or three-year-old seedlings in their nursery trays; four-year-old bulbs planted out in field nursery beds; five- or six-year-old bulbs flowering for the first time. Will there be a new and exciting variety among them?

successfully. If the seedlings' leaves are much bigger in the second year, then the bulbs should be lifted and potted in fresh compost once dormant again that summer. If the leaves are still thin and grass-like, it is best to wait another growing cycle before lifting the bulbs. Feeding with a weak solution of liquid tomato food will encourage the bulbs to get bigger. The small bulbs should then be lifted every year once dormant and re-potted in fresh compost. After four to seven years the bulbs should reach flowering size.

SEED PRODUCTION: DIFFERENCES BETWEEN SPECIES AND HYBRID TULIPS

Species

Some species will readily self-seed, and some are much shyer. Seed sown from species will come true if it has not crossed with a different species. In the wild, species tend to be isolated from one another and rarely have the chance to cross-pollinate, but as humans have collected various species from across the globe and brought them all into one place, this

has allowed for crosses that would otherwise not have occurred. The bulk of the tulips bought and sold today are hybrids and a result of many crosses over a long time.

Hybrids

Seed sown from most tulips apart from species, will not come out the same as the tulip the seed was collected from. Even if the pollination was strictly controlled to only allow self-fertilisation, the modern-day hybrids have a complicated set of genes acquired from many previous crosses and differences will be expressed in the resulting seeds. This, however, is what makes sowing tulip seeds very exciting; fantastic new varieties can be discovered. Indeed, it is this ease of crossing and subsequent differing flowers that has allowed so many wonderful tulip varieties to occur.

NEW VARIETIES

A new tulip variety can occur in two ways: either through the production of seeds or through random mutation in a bulb offset. Both require an amount of luck, although breeding new varieties from seed can be slightly more controlled through careful selection

Tulip breeding is a mixture of art, science and luck, but when you breed a new variety like this it is worth all the years of waiting in anticipation – Tulip 'Qatar', a new fringed double variety registered in 2021.

The anthers are removed from the other parent plant and the pollen from the paint brush is applied to the stigma.

of parent varieties. When two different species cross-pollinate, something that humans have facilitated by moving tulips into one place from different corners of the earth, the resulting seed will be a mix of genetical material from both parents. Some of the seeds may produce tulips that look just like either one of the parents, some maybe a combination of both parents, some however maybe completely different and have potential to be a worthwhile new variety.

Seeds

Breeding new varieties from seed starts by selecting two different varieties of tulips and allowing them to cross-pollinate, then following the steps above for growing the tulips on from the resulting seeds. This

Pollen is gathered from the anthers of one of the desired parent plants using a fine paint brush.

sounds quite easy and at a very basic level it is; however, commercial breeders take a much more structured approach that allows for some of the randomness to be controlled.

Not all tulip breeding is about creating brand new varieties – a good proportion is about improving existing varieties. For example, a breeder may have a batch of tulips grown from seeds that have produced a range of flowers with different traits. Some may have great flower colour but are lacking a sturdy stem, while others have a strong stem but a weak flower colour. By cross-pollinating these two examples, it is hoped that at least some of the resulting plants will gain both the positive traits and produce a much better variety. This is known as selective breeding.

Other reasons for selective breeding include:

- Stem length
- Flower longevity
- Disease resistance
- Bulb performance.

Most of the traits in the list are self-explanatory, but bulb performance requires a bit of explanation. Gardeners reading this book might be concerned with the performance of tulip bulbs in a garden setting, be that in the ground or in containers; therefore, buying bulbs of tulip varieties that have been bred to grow well in a garden setting would be advantageous. However, a large proportion of new tulip varieties have not been bred with this in mind. As discussed in the case study at the end of this chapter, breeding and bringing a new tulip variety to market is a lengthy process, somewhere in the region of twenty years. When that much time and money is invested, a breeder may want to cater for the biggest market possible which, as we see in chapter 9, is the cut flower market. A good cut flower variety does not always make a good garden variety, so while some of the new varieties can look amazing, older varieties that are still commercially available today are here because they have stood the test of time.

Tulip 'Strong Gold' is often used for breeding work due to its positive traits – good disease resistance and strong growth.

Tulip 'Purple Prince', a variety registered in 1987, has been used to breed a range of similar tulips in various colours that have proven good for cut flowers and the garden.

Mutations or sports

Previously, we stated that every bulblet that is produced will be the same as the parent bulb and, in theory, this should be the case. However, every now and again something causes the genes to behave differently, and an offset turns out to be different to the parent bulb. This is called a *mutation*, or a *sport* and some fantastic varieties have been established from this seemingly random occurrence. Tulip Couleur Cardinal is an old variety bred in 1845 that is still grown today, and a very good example of a variety that has created sports. There are multiple sports attributed to Tulip Couleur Cardinal, as can be seen in the three photos included on the next page. All are quite different; two maintain the original colouring, although one is a fringed tulip called Tulip Arma (1962), and the other is Tulip Rococo (1942), a Parrot tulip. The third sport has a completely different colour and is orange with a purple flame, Tulip Prinses Irene (1949). Prinses Irene has at least four sports of its own, although three of the four have very similar colours to the original Tulip Prinses Irene. Mutations are a random quirk of nature that may or may not occur, and we believe that is the way it should stay. However, people over the years have tried various methods to persuade the bulbs to change. Some of the best examples are from the

Tulip 'Couleur Cardinal' was first registered in 1845 and is still grown today, it is well known for its mutations or 'sports'. Many have been found quite randomly in the fields of this variety.

seventeenth century when tulip growers were trying to get their tulips to change from solid colours to flames and striped colours known as tulip 'breaking'; we discuss TBV a lot more in Chapter 3 and Chapter 8. Growers at the time tried various methods from pouring coloured potions into the soil where the tulips grew, to coating tulip bulbs in various substances. None of these methods had the desired effect. At the time they could not have known that a virus was the cause of the tulip changing colour. More recently, there has been research conducted in January 2021 in China that investigates the use of gamma radiation to effect mutations within tulips bulbs. While the research concludes that gamma radiation may have some use in creating tulip mutations, it is for scientists and breeders to debate the merits of this type of intervention in the breeding process.

Selective breeding, while based on tried-and-tested scientific methods, still requires a little luck to achieve results such as Tulip 'Striped Sail'. Previous generations tried various methods such as pouring food dye onto the soil to get colour combinations like this; most did not work.

Tulip 'Couleur Cardinal' has produced many 'sports'. From left to right (type and year of registration) Tulip 'Prinses Irene' (Dutch spelling) (Triumph, 1949), Tulip 'Arma' (Fringed, 1962), Tulip 'Rococo' (Parrot, 1942).

CHAPTER 5 CASE STUDY

Dutch tulip breeder Q&A

We have been asked many times before at flower shows if we have bred any tulip varieties, and our answer is invariably that we play no part in the breeding of tulips – we let the Dutch do what they are best at doing. We usually add that the breeding process itself is extremely involved and lengthy, better suited to either specialised companies or very dedicated tulip breeding hobbyists. Writing this chapter provided us with a great opportunity to meet a Dutch tulip breeder, find out more about the process of breeding and get answers to many of the tulip breeding-related questions that we had.

Joris van der Velden, of the Dutch breeding company Holland Bolroy Markt, comes from a family with a history in tulip growing and has himself been involved in tulip breeding for about thirty-five years. Across this time span, Joris thinks he has bred and named approximately 600 varieties of tulips. Although that

A conversation with Joris van der Velden, a Dutch tulip breeder, was a good case in point to re-emphasise just how involved the breeding process really is.

sounds like a very high number of new varieties, not all the newly bred varieties become commercially available. Approximately 150 varieties bred and named by Joris are now commercially available.

We had a few questions that were sparked both by our curiosity and by questions we have been asked ourselves by people interested in tulips. We felt that relating them in an informal interview format, which followed closely our dialogue with Joris during the tour of his trial grounds, would be the easiest way for readers to absorb this information.

Question: How long does it take to get to an entirely new tulip variety?

The answer was that approximately six or seven years was the length of time that would allow for creating a new variety and testing it, so as to ensure the genetic stability, behaviour and uniformity in the characteristics the breeding process sought to highlight. Once obtained, new varieties will be grown and monitored, and often remain unavailable commercially for a further ten years while bulb stocks are being increased.

Question: Why should gardeners plant tulip bulbs, rather than seeds?

Planting commercially available bulbs size 10–11cm (4–4½in) or larger in November or December will largely guarantee a display of blooms the following spring, which is why from a gardening perspective, bulbs are the quickest route to colourful displays. Starting from seeds planted in November, the result the following April will be seedlings resembling very thin and delicate blades of grass, which will take at least a further six years of nurturing before reaching a bulb size of 10–11cm (4–4½in) or larger.

Question: What is the average seed count in a pod, how long are seeds viable for and what is the germination rate?

There can be up to 250 seeds in each pod, but that can differ from one variety to another. In his trials, Joris only uses seeds produced earlier the same year; he does not use seeds that have been stored for over twelve months. The variability means that the germination rate can differ substantially from one variety to another, with some varieties producing far fewer seedlings than others. Joris is keen to point out, however, that every new seedling is precious, worth growing on and worth considering for selection.

Question: What does the breeding process involve?

Skill, experience and patience are of paramount importance when it comes to breeding tulips. Pollinating the stigma with the stamens is the active part of the breeding process that ensures that the seeds formed contain genetic material from both parents. The main tools used for this part of the

Tulip seedlings from seeds planted the previous autumn.

process are small paint brushes, string, scissors, tweezers and aluminium foil.

While the tools used are everyday items, the correct labelling and systematic record keeping, which includes full details of parentage, the year of breeding and the selection from first flowering are as important as the pollination in the breeding process.

It is possible to follow the process of pollination, growing the seeds, and selection on a smaller scale, or on an amateur basis, and in the Netherlands there continues to be a tulip-breeding tradition or hobby on a smaller scale. As long as the process is strictly adhered to, and seedlings are rigorously recorded and labelled, and the time investment is made, breeding as a hobby can produce successful results.

Question: What is the reason for breeding new tulip varieties?

There are a number of reasons for breeding new varieties. Enhancing characteristics desired of tulip plants is one of the main reasons for the breeding of new varieties. Disease resistance is also one of the sought-after characteristics, relevant for both garden varieties and for tulip varieties destined for the cut flower industry. The parent-varieties that the breeding will be centred on usually contain one or more characteristics that a new variety is expected to have. It may be that breeders look for new colour combinations, flower head shapes, or transposing well-established varieties into different tulip types, an example being Tulip Prinses Irene.

The equipment used for pollination is not quite as technical as one may expect.

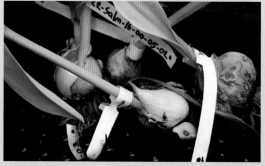

Labelling needs to continue to be accurate and rigorous throughout every stage of the process, including the stage where new bulbs form on selected plants.

Fresh from Joris' trial grounds, this is a new and currently unnamed tulip variety.

The codes on the labels in this picture have vital information, including details of the breeder, parentage, the year of breeding and the year of selection.

The majority of breeding happens in the context of market demand. In the tulip industry, the biggest proportion of tulips (approximately 80 per cent of the bulb production) goes into the cut flower industry, rather than garden growing varieties. Therefore, breeders look for new varieties that will withstand the fast-paced production process and behave well as cut flowers. For the cut flower industry, characteristics such as the length of the stem, shelf life and uprightness are equally important in breeding as colour, shape or height are for the garden varieties.

Question: How do you name new varieties?

Breeders tend to be concerned with the more pragmatic aspects of breeding, and outcomes of the process. It is true that some varieties have been named after grandparents and other members of the family who were involved in tulip growing and breeding, but the naming of new varieties is of secondary importance to obtaining varieties with the right characteristics, which are going to be suitable for market demand.

Three of many varieties bred by Joris that are all commercially available. Left to right: Tulip 'Candy Prince', Tulip 'Jan Seignette', Tulip 'Sunny Prince'.

TULIP VARIETIES

OLD OR NEW?

Often, when at flower shows, we are provided with the opportunity to speak to our customers about the tulip varieties we display and detail what we know about specific varieties in terms of when their flowering time is, any morphological particularities for the varieties such as colour changes into maturity, flower shape, flower opening and so on.

We are often asked whether varieties are old or new; gardeners are generally quite keen to try new varieties, while at the same time understanding the value and benefits of varieties that have stood the test of time. Hence the ensuing dilemma: should their purchase be one that is rational, and safe – an old variety – or should it be brave and adventurous – a new variety? We hesitate when it comes to recommending either new or old varieties but are very happy to share with customers and show visitors differences between old and new varieties that we are aware of. For the purpose of establishing the length of time in cultivation, we have added the year that the varieties described were registered in the Dutch tulip directory by their breeders.

VARIETIES: A SNAPSHOT IN TIME

Tulipa acuminata, one of the oldest varieties, was known in Turkey in the seventeenth century. The variety was appreciated for its slender and very pointy petals, as depicted in imagery of historical artefacts from the era. As interest in tulips and cultivation started its journey to Western Europe, the preference for the flower shape changed dramatically to much wider petals and more of a goblet shape, and further to the unusual patterns of flaming and feathering in the petals. It could thus be argued that different eras favoured different trends. But can the same be told of the current preferences of the public for a certain shape of tulip flower? In this section, we will list tulip varieties that we have grown successfully for many years. And indeed, as this section will show, the range of tulips available commercially includes every shape there is, and every colour. In today's tulip world, the wide variety of shapes, colours and types available is a result of careful preservation of some varieties and breeding to enhance certain characteristics in others. The multitude of tulip types available commercially can be attributed to the demand from gardeners on one hand, and the breeding of new varieties on the other hand. We argue that all tulip types have their place in the garden and deserve consideration.

EARLY FLOWERING TULIP VARIETIES (A-Z)

Tulip Exotic Emperor (White Valley)

A double-flowered, Fosteriana type, Tulip Exotic Emperor was registered in 2001. This variety grows up to 45cm (18in) in height. The colour of the petals is cream, delicately flanked by very thin sepals, giving the blooms a somewhat similar appearance to rose blooms.

Exotic Emperor is a tulip suitable for planting in beds, containers, and for using as a cut flower.

Tulip Flaming Purissima

A single-flowered, Fosteriana type, Tulip Flaming Purissima grows up to 45cm (18in) in height. The petals are coloured cream at the base on the exterior, flamed on the whole surface of the petal with delicate, pink striations.

Tulip Flaming Purissima grows well in the ground and in containers. It was registered in 1999.

Tulip Giuseppe Verdi

A single-flowered, Kaufmanniana type, Tulip Giuseppe Verdi is a well-established, long-standing tulip, having been registered in 1955, and one of the recognised short varieties, growing up to 30cm (12in) in height. The colour of the petals is red on the outside and yellow on the inside. The flowers open wide in the sun, obscuring the red on the exterior when flowers are fully open.

Tulip 'Exotic Emperor'.

Tulip 'Flaming Purissima'.

Tulip 'Giuseppe Verdi'.

Tulip 'Monsella'.

Tulip Monsella

Double Early-flowered, Tulip Monsella has bright yellow petals with fine red lines in the middle of the petals, both on the inside and on the outside, making Tulip Monsella one of the brightest early varieties.

A relatively short variety, at 30–35cm (12–14in) Tulip Monsella is suitable for planting in the ground in borders and for bedding. It was registered in 1981.

Tulip Pinocchio

A single-flowered, Greigii type, Tulip Pinocchio was registered in 1980 and is a short variety, 20–25cm (8–10in) in height with pink petals delicately edged with a white stripe.

Tulip Pinocchio is particularly well-suited to growing in containers.

Tulip 'Pinocchio'.

Tulip Scarlet Baby

A great multi-stemmed variety, Tulip Scarlet Baby is a Kaufmanniana type ideal for rockeries, low containers, or planted as very early bedding. Tulip Scarlet Baby is one of the shortest varieties, growing to approximately 20cm (8in).

The flowers are intense scarlet when the buds colour up, but as they mature, they brighten up with fiery reds or dark orange tinges. Tulip Scarlet Baby was registered in 1962.

Tulip Sweetheart

A single-flowered, Fosteriana type, Tulip Sweetheart is an early flowering variety that grows to 40cm (16in). The colour of the petals is cream, heavily flushed with a yellowish, buttery lower half of the flower. The lighter

Tulip 'Sweetheart'.

Tulip 'Scarlet Baby'.

cream top part of the petals lightens further as the flowers age.

Tulip Sweetheart can be grown in beds, containers, and for using as a cut flower. It was registered in 1976.

Tulip The First

True to its name, Tulip The First can often be in flower even as long as one month before other early-flowering varieties. A Kaufmanniana type, Tulip The First will bring a splash of colour to borders very early in the season, sometimes as early as the end of February.

As well as in borders, Tulip The First performs equally well when planted in containers, with a height of approximately 30cm (12in). Tulip The First was registered in 1940, making it one of the more established tulip varieties.

Tulip 'The First'.

Tulip 'Abu Hassan'.

MID-SEASON FLOWERING TULIP VARIETIES (A-Z)

Tulip Abu Hassan

Registered in 1976, and a single-flowered Triumph-type, Tulip Abu Hassan is a mid-season flowering tulip that grows to mid-height, approximately 45cm (18in). Delicately gold-edged copper-coloured petals are unique in the tulip range of colours, reminiscent of Middle Eastern spices.

This is a very attractive and popular variety, which grows well when planted in the ground in sunny locations.

Tulip Agrass White

A single-flowered, slightly off-white, Triumph-type that grows to 45cm (18in) high, Tulip Agrass White was registered in 1997, and is a favourite variety for white gardens early in the season. Unlike other white tulips,

Tulip 'Agrass White'.

the flower maintains a goblet shape when fully open with more pointed than rounded petals.

Tulip Agrass White is a popular variety as a cut flower and for wedding flowers.

Tulip Apeldoorn

Tulip Apeldoorn, which was registered in 1951, is a single-flowered, orangey-red, Darwin type that grows to 55–60cm (22–24in) high. Tulip Apeldoorn has a large flower head with the top of the petals forming a straight edge. Tulip Apeldoorn and Tulip Golden Apeldoorn are easily recognised because of the black centre with the yellow rim on the inside, at the base of the petals.

Named after a place in Holland, Apeldoorn is one of the older Darwin types, most reliable and still popular varieties, often seen in large planting schemes in parks. Over fifteen new varieties of tulips have been attributed to mutations from Tulip Apeldoorn.

Tulip Apricot Foxx

Salmon pink with a wide apricot edge, Tulip Apricot Foxx is a relatively recent variety from the Triumph type, registered in 2009, which grows to approximately 50cm (20in).

A good garden variety, Tulip Apricot Foxx is also very popular as a cut flower and for flower arrangements due to its modern colour combination and attractive flower shape.

Tulip Banja Luka

Registered in 1998, Tulip Banja Luka is a more modern Darwin Hybrid, with a robust growing habit and reliability typical of other Darwin Hybrid varieties.

Growing up to 55cm (22in), with a large flower head, Banja Luka combines the fiery colours red and yellow, with the red being the primary colour, with

Tulip 'Apeldoorn'.

Tulip 'Apricot Foxx'.

Tulip 'Banja Luka'.

Tulip 'Candy Prince'.

feathered yellow edges and some yellow flaming. Particularly good to perennialise in optimum growing conditions.

Tulip Candy Prince

Part of the Single Early group, the 'Candy' range of tulips, which includes Tulip Candy Prince, has several distinguishing features: they are of medium height, growing to approximately 30–35cm (12–14in), with sturdy stems. The flowers maintain a closed shape and are unusually long lasting, with petals holding their shape until the very end of the flowering period.

Several other varieties within this range display the same features, mainly the longevity of the flower, making them suitable for more exposed locations and for planting in public displays. Tulip Candy Prince was registered in 2001.

Tulip Daydream

A single-flowered Darwin Hybrid, Tulip Daydream grows up to 60cm (24in) in height. The colour intensifies as the plants mature, changing from a lemon shade in the initial stages of flowering, through to orange as the flowers mature.

Daydream is suitable for planting in beds, borders, and for using as a cut flower. Somewhat unusually, on sunny spring days, Tulip Daydream sends out a mild, very pleasant scent. Tulip Daydream was added to the tulip register in 1980.

Tulip Flaming Flag

A member of the Triumph group, Tulip Flaming Flag is a tall variety, reaching to 50–55cm (20–22in). One of the more recent additions to the tulip register in 2007,

Tulip 'Daydream'.

Tulip 'Flaming Flag'.

the primary colour is white, with a thin flaming of purple, which transitions into softer, paler purple tones.

The distinctive and strong contrast between white and purple makes this variety particularly recognisable and striking in appearance. Suitable for growing in the garden and also for cut flowers.

Tulip Foxtrot

Part of the Double Early group, and registered in 2000, Tulip Foxtrot is soft pink and white. Sometimes a green flushing on the outer petals can be observed. A relatively short variety, growing up to 35cm (14in), Tulip Foxtrot is particularly well suited to bedding displays, but also as a cut flower.

Following the popularity of this variety, Tulip White Foxtrot was registered in 2020 and Tulip Pink Foxtrot in

Tulip 'Foxtrot'.

2021, some of the most recent additions to the Dutch tulip register.

Tulip Golden Apeldoorn

Tulip Golden Apeldoorn is single flowered, believed to have been registered between 1951–1960, and is a vibrant yellow, Darwin type that grows to 55–60cm (22–24in) high. Tulip Golden Apeldoorn has a large flower head with the top of the petals forming a straight edge when mature. Tulip Apeldoorn and Tulip Golden Apeldoorn are easily recognised because of the black centre with the yellow rim on the inside, at the base of the petals.

Named after a place in Holland, Tulip Apeldoorn is one of the older Darwin types; reliable and still popular, it is often seen in large planting schemes in parks.

Tulip Hemisphere

Tulip Hemisphere is part of the Triumph group. It was registered in 2000, making it a relatively recent variety and is of medium height, growing to approximately 40cm (16in). Tulip Hemisphere is an unusual variety due to the changes in colour throughout the flowering period. Flowers start off very light – nearly white – and as they mature, they flush with pink up to the stage of becoming entirely pink.

Although planted at the same time, a cluster of Tulip Hemisphere will look very non-uniform in colour, displaying a spectrum from white, to flushed, to deep pink, depending on how advanced the flowering process.

Tulip 'Golden Apeldoorn'.

Tulip 'Hemisphere'.

Tulip Inzell

A Triumph-type, Tulip Inzell was registered in 1969 and is a medium-height tulip, mainly white with a just perceptible pink flushing through the outside of the petals – only visible at very close inspection.

Similarly to Tulip Agrass White, Tulip Inzell is a popular variety for wedding flowers and for pastel colour combinations, growing well in planted beds and containers to a height of 45cm (18in).

Tulip Jimmy

Despite being a relatively old Triumph variety, Tulip Jimmy, registered in 1962, grows to 35–40cm (14–16in) and has a surprisingly contemporary colour combination. The pink petals are edged with a medium width orange stripe.

With medium size flowers with stems that are short to medium length, Tulip Jimmy grows well in the ground and in containers.

Tulip 'Jimmy'.

Tulip Kees Nelis

Tulip Kees Nelis, a Triumph variety registered in 1951, can be considered one of the varieties that has stood the test of time. With red flowers edged with a medium

Tulip 'Inzell'.

Tulip 'Kees Nelis'.

yellow band and a goblet shape to the flower, Tulip Kees Nelis grows to 45cm (18in) and is a reliable variety for growing in the garden and for cut flowers.

Tulip Leen van der Mark

Similarly, Tulip Leen van der Mark is a Triumph variety registered in 1968, with a similar height (45cm/18in), shape and coloration pattern, the main difference being the outer band to the petals, which is a bright cream as the flowers mature, rather than yellow.

Tulip Pallada

Tulip Pallada is a Triumph-type registered in 1997, which is very close to what many people think of as a traditional red tulip. Quite short and sturdy-stemmed, Tulip Pallada grows to 34–40cm (14–16in) and is well-suited to being grown in the ground and in containers in windier locations.

Tulip 'Pallada'.

Tulip 'Leen van der Mark'.

Tulip Prinses Irene

Tulip Prinses Irene (Princess Irene), which is a Triumph variety, is a mutation from Tulip Couleur Cardinal, which was selected and registered as a stand-alone variety in 1949. Like many other Triumph category

Tulip 'Prinses Irene'.

tulips, Tulip Prinses Irene is quite short, growing to 35–40cm (14–16in). The contrast between the toned-down orange and the purple flaming through the middle on the outside of the petal continues to make it one of the most popular tulip varieties.

Tulip Purissima

Tulip Purissima is a Fosteriana type registered in 1943, which starts off creamy in colour and matures to a lighter white. It is a slightly taller variety, growing to 45cm (18in), often used in wedding flowers, which suits being grown in containers or in the ground.

Tulip Purple Prince

Tulip Purple Prince is a Single Early type registered in 1987, and is fairly short-stemmed, growing to 35cm (14in). Similarly to other varieties from the 'Prince'

Tulip 'Purple Prince'.

range, Tulip Purple Prince is particularly long-lasting when it flowers and it maintains a closed goblet shape throughout the flowering period.

Tulip Rococo

Tulip Rococo, similarly to Prinses Irene, is a mutation from Tulip Couleur Cardinal identified, selected and registered in 1942. Unlike Tulip Prinses Irene, Tulip Rococo is a Parrot tulip, with the recognisable blueish flushing on the outside of the petal, but with specific Parrot-type petals that are crinkled at the edges alongside a straight centre. Rococo grows to 35cm (14in) in height.

Tulip Ronaldo

Tulip Ronaldo, a more recently registered Triumph-type (1997) is intense burgundy in colour and has a velvety quality imparted by its colour. Well suited to

Tulip 'Purissima'.

Tulip 'Rococo'.

growing in containers and in the ground, Tulip 'Ronaldo' offers a great contrasting colour for planting schemes, growing to approximately 50cm (20in).

Tulip Shirley

Tulip Shirley is a popular Triumph-type tulip, growing to 50cm (20in) in height. The flowers start with a creamy colour and as they mature, the thin purple edging to the petals and spots on the petals become more and more intense in colour. Tulip Shirley is an example of a tulip where the name of the variety makes it more sought after.

Tulip Sunny Prince

Tulip Sunny Prince is a Single Early type from the Prince range, registered in 2002, and fairly short stemmed, growing to 30–35cm (12–14in). Similarly to other varieties from the 'Prince' range, Tulip Sunny Prince is

Tulip 'Ronaldo'.

Tulip 'Shirley'.

Tulip 'Sunny Prince'.

Tulip 'Tom Pouce'.

particularly long-lasting when it flowers and it main-tains a closed goblet shape throughout the flowering period. The colour of the flowers is a toned-down lemon colour when the flowers mature.

Tulip Tom Pouce

One of the newer varieties, Tom Pouce is a Triumph-type tulip registered in 2000. The outside base of the petals is creamy-yellow, fusing through the pink of the rest of the petals. A taller Triumph-type tulip, growing to 45–50cm (18–20in), Tulip Tom Pouce performs well in the ground and in containers and it is well suited for cut flowers.

Tulip Van Eijk

Tulip Van Eijk is a tall Darwin variety registered in 1995. Its unique silvery-pink colour, height of 50cm (20in) and relatively large flower head makes it a well-suited variety for mass planting displays or in large flower beds. Due to its features, it has been used in breeding programmes in recent times.

Tulip 'Van Eijk'.

Tulip 'Verandi'.

Tulip Verandi

Tulip Verandi, a Triumph-type tulip registered in 1999, would look like the archetypal red tulip, were it not for the very delicate golden edges around the petals. The edging of the petals accentuates the goblet shape of the flowers. Growing to 50cm (20in), Verandi is well suited to growing in the garden or using as a cut flower.

LATE-FLOWERING TULIP VARIETIES (A-Z)

Tulip Aladdin

Tulip Aladdin is a Lily-flowered variety registered in 1942. Tulip Aladdin is a tall variety growing to 55cm (22in) and has a very elegant appearance with slender reflexed petals. The white edging of the petals accentuates the pointy shape and the sense of elegance. Always a very popular variety with the public, Tulip Aladdin has a fairy tale name alongside an exquisite look.

Tulip Ballerina

A Lily-flowering type, Tulip Ballerina was registered in 1980. Similar to Tulip Aladdin, Tulip Ballerina grows up to 60cm (24in) in height. The colour of the petals is

Tulip 'Aladdin'.

Tulip 'Ballerina'.

orange, and the slender shape specific to the lily-flowered type makes it very apt for the name of the variety.

Always a very popular variety in show exhibits, Tulip Ballerina is suitable for planting in beds and for using as a cut flower.

Tulip Blue Diamond

Tulip Blue Diamond is a Double Late type registered in 1990. Tulip Blue Diamond is a relatively tall double tulip, growing to 40–45cm (16–18in). Double tulips are also referred to as peony-type tulips. The weight of the flower head can be difficult to support on the tall stem when mature, making Tulip Blue Diamond a very good variety for cut flowers.

Tulip Blue Parrot

Tulip Blue Parrot is part of the Parrot group, with the exact registration date of this variety not being known,

Tulip 'Blue Parrot'.

but understood to be pre-1935. The two things that stand out about this variety are that, despite the name 'Blue', the colour is actually lilac, or mauve. There is no known naturally blue tulip variety. Secondly, the crinkling of the petals is less pronounced in this variety, and the serration of the edge of the petals largely absent, making Blue Parrot resemble a double-flowered variety rather than a Parrot. Nonetheless, Tulip Blue Parrot is a very attractive variety that grows to 50cm (20in) in the garden and in containers.

Tulip Crème Upstar

Tulip Crème Upstar is a Double Late type, which was registered in 1994. The stems for this variety tend to be quite short and sturdy, up to 30–35cm (12–14in), which means that they remain upright and do not struggle with the weight of the flower head. Tulip Crème Upstar is well suited to growing in containers and in the ground.

Tulip Doll's Minuet

Registered in 1968, Tulip Doll's Minuet is one of the later Lily-flowered type tulips. Specific to the group, Tulip Doll's Minuet has very pointy and slender petals. In addition to other tulip varieties from this category, Tulip Doll's Minuet also has the green flushing on the outside

Tulip 'Blue Diamond'.

Tulip 'Crème Upstar'.

of the petals specific to Viridiflora-type tulips. Tulip Doll's Minuet grows to approximately 50cm (20in).

Tulip Flaming Spring Green

Tulip Flaming Spring Green is a Viridiflora-type tulip registered in 1999. An addition of red flaming in the middle of the petals on the inside, combined with the specific Viridiflora feature of green flushing on the outside petals leads to spectacular results. Tulip Flaming Spring Green is a tall variety that grows well when planted in the ground and in containers to a height of 50cm (22in).

Tulip Pretty Love

Tulip Pretty Love is one of the newest Lily-flowered type tulips, registered in 2011. In terms of flower shape,

Tulip 'Doll's Minuet'.

Tulip 'Flaming Spring Green'.

Tulip 'Pretty Love'.

Tulip 'Queen of Night'.

Tulip Pretty Love is much more akin to the more recently devised Coronet group, with the ends of the petals bearing the pinched resemblance and forming the crown shape. Intense pink in colour, Tulip Pretty Love is an upright, medium-height variety that grows to approximately 40cm (16in).

Tulip Queen of Night

Tulip Queen of Night is a part of the Single Late group, and without a doubt one of the most-well established and popular tulip varieties. Registered pre-1944, Tulip Queen of Night is very tall, easily getting to 55–60cm (22–24in) in the right conditions. While the flower head size may not be the biggest, Tulip Queen of Night is an excellent variety to use for spot planting; it performs well when planted in the ground.

Tulip Spring Green

Part of the Viridiflora group, Tulip Spring Green was first registered in 1969. Quite a tall variety, reaching 50–55cm (20–22in), Tulip Spring Green is the best

Tulip 'Spring Green'.

example of a Viridiflora-type tulip, with the green flushing on the outside of the petals abundantly obvious. Tulip Spring Green is a good variety for white, monochromatic gardens.

Tulip Texas Flame

Tulip Texas Flame is part of the Parrot group and was registered in 1958. It is a good example of a variety that presents cross-group features, with the clear features of a Parrot tulip including the crinkled petals with serrated edges, but in addition, it features the green flushing on the outside. Tulip Texas Flame is quite a tall variety, getting to 50–55cm (20–22in). The flower head can sometimes become too heavy if the stem loses turgescence due to underwatering. As with most Parrot-type tulip varieties, Tulip Texas Flame is very well suited for cut flowers.

Tulip Uncle Tom

Tulip Uncle Tom was registered pre-1939, making it one of the most long-lasting double tulip varieties. It is part of the Double Late group and the intense burgundy-coloured flower resembles the shape of peony or ranunculus flowers. Although relatively short, growing to approximately 35–40cm (14–16in), due to the weight of the flower head, Tulip Uncle Tom works well as a cut flower or as part of flower arrangements.

Tulip West Point

Tulip West Point is part of the Lily-flowered group and was registered in 1943. Very typical of the other varieties

Tulip 'Uncle Tom'.

Tulip 'Texas Flame'.

Tulip 'Westpoint'.

from this group, the very pointy petals are reminiscent of *Tulipa acuminata*, as discussed in the case study from Chapter 1. Tulip West Point is a tall variety that grows to 50cm (22in), well suited to being planted in the ground.

Tulip Witte Rebel

A relative new addition to the Tulip register in 1999, Witte Rebel (or White Rebel in English) is part of the Parrot group. Similarly to other varieties from this group, especially in the earlier stages of flowering, it is easy to distinguish a green flushing on the outside of the petals. Tulip White Rebel with its contemporary and artistic appearance, can get tall at 40–45cm (16–18in), and top heavy, making it a well-suited variety for cut flowers.

Tulip White Triumphator

Tulip White Triumphator is part of the Lily-flowered group and was registered in 1942. It is a tall variety growing to approximately 55cm (22in) in height, with the petals somewhat wider and less pointy than other tulips from this category. Tulip White Triumphator is well suited for growing in the ground.

Tulip 'Witte Rebel'.

Tulip 'White Triumphator'.

CHAPTER 6 CASE STUDY

Varieties that have stood the test of time

Many gardeners recognise tulips as a mainstay throughout their lives. We often remember tulips from childhood, not least because of their very recognisable features in terms of shape and colour. But when we think of the red tulips we remember from childhood, can they be the same red tulips that we grow now, or was it that we remember the vibrancy of the colour? The chances are that they could be the same varieties that our parents, and maybe even our grandparents, grew in their gardens.

As we discuss in the following chapter, there continue to be in existence historic varieties that were bred in the sixteenth or seventeenth centuries. There are very few historic varieties left, which are painstakingly maintained as part of a collection at Hortus Bulborum in the Netherlands, such as Duc van Tol Red and Yellow (1595), Duc van Tol Orange (1700), Amiral de Constantinople (1722) or Silver Standard (1760), but when talking about varieties that have stood the test of time, it is not the historic varieties that we have in mind; only very few bulbs from those varieties are kept cultivated, mainly because of the commitment of groups of volunteers from Hortus Bulborum. What we have in mind are tulip varieties registered from the mid-1800s to the mid-1900s that continue to be in cultivation on a large scale and available commercially; in other words, the tulip varieties that perhaps our grandparents, parents and ourselves have planted in our gardens.

Tulip 'Amiral de Constantinople' is a historic variety that is still in existence in a handful of collections. But when talking here about varieties that have stood the test of time, we refer to commercially available varieties.

By and large, varieties that have stood the test of time tend to be of solid colour. As explained previously, the petal discoloration resulting in flaming and feathering patterns that made those tulip varieties very much sought-after during Tulipmania were caused by Tulip Breaking Virus (TBV). This, in turn, made the bulb stock weaker and it largely led to the demise of some varieties. This provides a good explanation as to why many of the longest standing varieties are of solid colour.

To illustrate tulips that have stood the test of time, we selected three of our favourite varieties that belong to three different classes: Tulip Couleur Cardinal, Tulip Peach Blossom and Tulip Orange Favourite.

Tulip Couleur Cardinal

Registered in 1845, the Triumph-type Tulip Couleur Cardinal continues to fascinate through its intense, deep red, flushed on the outside middle of the petals with a blue tint. Performing really well in the garden and in containers, Couleur Cardinal has a relatively shorter stem, which makes it better at withstanding windy conditions.

As explained in Chapter 5, Couleur Cardinal has produced a number of mutations, which have since been selected and established as new varieties in their own right. It continues to be grown on a large scale, with eight hectares being planted in the Netherlands with bulbs of this variety in 2021.

Tulip Peach Blossom

Registered in 1890 by H.N. van Leeuwen, Tulip Peach Blossom looks surprisingly contemporary for a variety bred over 130 years ago. A Double Early variety, Peach Blossom is a deep rose-coloured variety that grows to approximately 25cm (10in), very similar in shape to a peony flower.

Excellent for planting in the garden, containers and for use in flower arranging, Tulip Peach Blossom will always be on our list of recommended tulip varieties.

Tulip Orange Favourite

Registered in 1930 by K.C. Vooren, Orange Favourite is a tall, Parrot-type tulip. In the early stages of flowering, the flowers have a salmony-pink tint, flushed with green on the outside of the petal, which matures to a brilliant orange as the flowering progresses. Tulip Orange Favourite is a mildly scented variety that was awarded the Highly Commended status by the RHS in 1982.

It is also a tulip crossing over different types, displaying clear features of parrot tulips with the

Tulip 'Couleur Cardinal'.

Tulip 'Peach Blossom'.

feathered textured edges, but also Viridiflora features with the green flushing running on the outside of the petals. The overall artistic appearance of Tulip Orange Favourite, equally contemporary-looking to Tulip Peach Blossom goes a long way in explaining this variety's continued popularity.

There are many more tulip varieties that have been bred and registered a long time before many of us were born. Being aware of the length of time some of the current varieties have been in cultivation might give us pause to reflect on how many previous generations have marvelled at the same spectacle next time we see a tulip display.

Tulip 'Orange Favourite'.

TULIP GARDENS AND PLACES OF INTEREST

A lot has been published about tulips from all-encompassing perspectives, which include history, botany, taxonomy, science, garden design and photography. Indeed, publications such as *The Tulip Anthology* (2010) edited by Billie Lythberg are an outstanding example of factual content, photography and poetry centred around tulips. The importance of all these publications should not be underestimated. New tulip varieties, new knowledge in terms of cultivation, new understanding and new interpretations of history mean that the subject of tulips is an ever-fascinating one.

It is, however, true to say that the value and impact of seeing tulip fields and tulip gardens in real life, at a time of the year when there is no other genus that offers the breadth of colours and shapes is at least equal to, if not more than that of published information. We take the opportunity in this section to introduce readers to several places in England and elsewhere in Europe and further afield, where displays of tulips enchant the public in the spring. For this, we have selected public spaces and private gardens of different sizes, which are open to the public and are well known for their tulip displays.

The aim of this section is not to compare or rank places where tulips can be admired, but rather, to highlight the different scales at which tulips are displayed for the public and to offer tulip enthusiasts

willing to travel some suggestions of perhaps unexpected places in the north of England, Europe and elsewhere in the world where tulips in bloom can be admired. By no means an exhaustive list, these are some locations that the authors have visited and some that we are aware of, and are happy to recommend to other gardeners.

TULIP GARDENS IN THE UK

Constable Burton Hall, North Yorkshire

Constable Burton Hall is a Georgian property located in Constable Burton, North Yorkshire. The property, which is privately owned, is set in extensive grounds that include a historic woodland and walled garden on the north side of the estate, and formal gardens to the west of the property. Although included in this section of our book as a destination to see tulips for its yearly Tulip Festival, the gardens at Constable Burton Hall have much more to offer: the garden trail winds its way around the estate from the Sundial Garden through to the Terrace Garden, the Cedars of Lebanon, Granny's Garden, Acer Walk, the Rock Garden, the Park Walk and Beck area, the Reflection Ponds, the Lime Avenue and the Daffodil Field.

Constable Burton Hall in North Yorkshire is a privately owned property with large grounds and gardens. The gardens are open to the public in the spring and summer. A tulip festival has been a yearly event in their spring calendar for over twenty years.

The Tulip Festival has been running for over twenty years and every year, thousands of tulip bulbs are planted in the autumn and produce spectacular displays in the spring, with over 7,000 bulbs estimated to have been planted for the last tulip festival. The event is sponsored by Bloms Bulbs, who provide a wide selection of bulbs including some old favourites and new varieties. The Wyvill family with Andrew Moss, the Head Gardener at Constable Burton, decide together on planting schemes and locations for the following year's event.

The formal gardens nearer the house – particularly the Sundial Garden and the Terrace Garden – are where many of the tulips are displayed in the spring, when the gardens are open to the public on designated dates.

The chosen method of displaying the tulips at Constable Burton Hall is predominantly in spacious planted beds, with the exception of planting near the walled garden section near the top of the Lime Avenue, where there are several tulip varieties planted in single variety clusters.

Due to its vast expanse and multiple features – be they determined by the landscape or built structures – the different locations in the garden, with their specific microclimates offer a good example of what stage the flowering is at, depending on how sunny and sheltered the location is. As discussed in Chapter 4, the sections of the garden that are situated nearer the house, such as the Sundial Garden, the Terrace Garden and the old

Long borders planted with various tulip varieties, often mixed to give a long season of interest.

The walled garden at the top of the Lime Avenue lends itself to clumps of tulips being planted among the emerging herbaceous plants. Tulip 'Apricot Beauty' (left), Tulip 'Verona' (right).

walled garden provide a sheltered area, where the built environment forms a suntrap, are the places where first tulips come into flower. Conversely, the north-facing lawns leading onto the entrance of the property house tulips beds, which are the last to flower. The gardens, with their multitude of locations available to plant tulips, thus allow for an extended display. At the same time, this is a good visual cue that illustrates the effect of orientation of a planting space on the flowering period, which becomes more of a concern when space is limited, and influences the choice of what can be planted.

The tulip displays at Constable Burton Hall are a definite must-see for any tulip afficionados, and one of the reasons for this is the bold mix of varieties in some of the borders. Some of the tulip beds include a variety of colours within similar tulip types, and other beds include unexpected and impressive combinations of different tulip types mixed together – Darwin type, Double flowering tulips, Lily-flowered types and Parrot tulips. We thought this was a very inspiring example of experimenting and not conforming to expectations. The scale of the space is not dissimilar to the scale of historic continental European properties; however,

A wide range of mixed varieties are planted in flower beds at Constable Burton, creating a dramatic feature among the established shrubs and trees.

A unique addition to the tulip festival at Constable Burton is the cut flower display of tulips exhibited by Bloms Bulbs.

existing mature trees mean there are many other features to be admired in the gardens at Constable Burton Hall. Yet, where tulips are concerned at Constable Burton Hall, experimentation with designs including planted beds with a wide variety of tulip types and heights have a very impactful effect, with the added benefit of the diversity of shapes, colours and textures, which focuses attention and encourages the exploration of differences – a more stimulating means to enjoying tulips than merely admiring them.

From this point of view, the displays at Constable Burton Hall reinforced the fact that colour mixes do not cause any detriment to the design, but rather, they enhance its vibrancy and energy. In addition to the planted displays, the Tulip Festival at Constable Burton Hall has the added benefit for the visitors of displays of cut tulip flowers, all grouped in named varieties. There are very few places within the UK that offer this type of tulip display, with Bloms being the only other company offering a cut flower display at the RHS Chelsea Flower Show in London.

Gresgarth Hall Gardens, North Lancashire

Situated northeast of Lancaster, in Lancashire, Gresgarth Hall Gardens was until recently one of the best-kept secrets of the north. In 2020 Gresgarth Hall Gardens rose to prominence after winning the Historic

Tulip 'Claudia' grown in a container on the terrace in front of the main house, Gresgarth Hall. Like all the lily-flowered tulips, its pointed petals make an elegant statement befitting of the house.

Gresgarth Hall in Lancashire is surrounded by an immaculately maintained, twelve-acre mature garden.

Houses Garden of the Year: Judge's Choice Award (for gardens), making it one of the most-visited gardens in the region.

In its entirety of twelve acres of cultivated land, Gresgarth Hall Gardens is nothing short of spectacular. Not mentioning the fact that interest in any aspect of gardening and landscaping would be more than satisfied at Gresgarth would not do justice to the place. From the immaculate walled kitchen garden, to the lake and water gardens in front of the terraces, through to the masterfully chosen and executed planting around the house and on the terraces, and through to the ample dendrologic value and showcase of rare specimens, Gresgarth Hall Gardens offers awe and excitement to visitors at every turn, regardless of the time of year.

As regards tulips, the gardens offer, in our view, a unique insight into potential and endless possibilities of tulips grown in containers. In spring, the terraces are adorned with oversize terracotta containers, which contain combinations of different tulip varieties and other spring-flowering plants. The colour combinations are bold and full of the energy of spring, with inspired underplanting, which makes for complete ensembles, as shown in the photograph. It is easy to underestimate the extent to which the vibrancy of colour can highlight and emphasise particularities in certain places or spaces such as terraces.

Undeniably, the overall background and the context plays a very important role at Gresgarth Hall Gardens. But if inspiration is to be drawn and adapted to other contexts, the approach to growing containerised tulips at Gresgarth is one of the most inspiring examples of how gardening magic can be created in containers by anyone, even when a full size garden is not available, thereby highlighting the accessibility of tulip growing. Planting combinations include different coloured tulips and other spring-flowering bulbs such as

A repurposed copper container left from the old mill previously located at Gresgarth Hall is planted with Tulip 'Queen of Night', Tulip 'Gavota' and *Fritillaria imperialis* 'Rubra'.

Beautifully thought out and planted containers on the terrace below Gresgarth Hall with bold colour combinations and well-selected underplanting.

Fritillaria Imperialis 'Rubra'. We also noted different material containers such as copper pots, repurposed from past mill work.

Another unique feature at Gresgarth is the spring planting under the pleached lime walk. It can be argued that the planting style in the section of the garden defies understanding of how tulips are best planted, and demonstrates that nothing should be set in stone. It is true that planting of tulips bulbs close together is believed to be offer the greatest impact. However, where sufficient knowledge and confidence are involved, a wild, naturalised look involving tulip hybrids can also be achieved.

Gresgarth Hall Gardens is open to the public from February to November, on the second Sunday of the month.

Here, a half wooden barrel has been used for a tulip display, underplanted with white forget-me-not, with a combination of *Narcissus* 'Thalia' and Tulip 'Spring Green' behind.

It is possible to achieve an effortless spring meadow feel with a combination of cowslips (*Primula veris*), bluebells (*Hyacinthoides nonscripta*) and anemones (*Anemone blanda*), dotted with Tulip 'Queen of Night' and Tulip 'Purple Flag'.

Bayntun Flowers, Wiltshire

An equally inspiring destination for tulips is Bayntun Flowers, in the village of Blackland, near Calne in Wiltshire. Bayntun Flowers, owned and curated by Polly Nicholson, is only open for the public on designated open days advertised on their website and for workshops, which must be booked in advance.

The idyllic setting of the walled garden and the coach house within the surrounding Blackland fields is home not only to an exquisite artisan flower grower and florist, but also to the only private national collections of historic tulips in England, as listed in the

Plant Heritage's national plant collections. Historic tulips, including 'flamed' and 'feathered' tulip varieties are very few and far between, with only one tulip society maintaining bulbs of historic varieties, and organising an annual show, as detailed in the case study for Chapter 8. Polly Nicholson's collection comprises seventy-eight individual cultivars grown in stock beds located in a field near the walled garden and in containers within the walled garden. For tulip enthusiasts and the general public alike, the promise of so many different cultivars of English Florists' Tulips and Dutch historic tulips all in one place is a tremendously exciting proposition, and seeing this collection

The walled garden at Bayntun Flowers is the perfect location to showcase Polly Nicholson's fondness for tulips and historic garden traditions.

in person on one of the organised open days is a must.

In addition to beautiful, oversized terracotta containers planted up with tulip varieties that are complementary in their colour range, and vibrant tulip planted beds near the steps down from the coach house, the immaculately refurbished walled garden displays an assembly of gardening techniques with outstanding results: step-over trained fruit trees edge planted beds, espalier-trained trees line the inner walls of the garden and topiary trees provide structure and focus. Thoughtful inclusion of willow structures, vintage garden furniture and repurposed vintage containers complete the style. The sense of value attributed to traditional gardens and that of applying historic gardening principles is pervasive throughout at Bayntun Flowers.

Outside the walled garden there are ample opportunities provided to see naturalised tulips in the grass

Tulips can be grown in any shape or size container, but repurposing previously used farm objects create a superb vintage appearance.

A joyous display of colour and form, which includes *Tulipa acuminata*, Tulip 'Ballerina' and Tulip 'Queen of Night' is a good example of naturalised tulip planting at Bayntun Flowers.

bed along the exterior wall of the walled garden and peeping through the wild meadow-style planted bank opposite the entrance to the coach house. Tulips are encouraged to settle freely within the less formal environment outside the walled garden. Where necessary, the numbers are supplemented by additional tulip bulbs planted in the autumn. No less impressive than the garden itself is the vast collection of repurposed containers, including metal water troughs and metal barrels, which line the exterior walls of the garden and that, at the time of our visit, were planted up with the most inspiring combinations of tulip varieties.

Aesthetics and form are not the only features that prompted us to include Bayntun Flowers as a destination to see tulips; the philosophy underpinning growing for the garden and the flowers used for arrangements and to supply florists make Bayntun Flowers stand out. Everything is grown organically, in accordance with the Soil Association certification granted. At a time when environmental concerns filter through every aspect of gardening, it is inspiring to see the possibilities and results of organic growing that Bayntun Flowers achieves.

Polly Nicholson's historic tulip collection: a rare sight of 'flames' and 'feathers'.

OTHER TULIP COLLECTIONS IN ENGLAND

Cambridge University Botanic Gardens

Specifically focused on species tulips, Cambridge University Botanic Gardens is home to a collection of approximately sixty species, which was recognised by the Ministry of Agriculture after the Second World War but had existed and been curated around twenty years prior.

Maintained mainly as a pot-grown collection in the Mountains House part of their glasshouse range, the species tulips in the Cambridge University Botanic Gardens collection can be admired from February through to May.

https://www.botanic.cam.ac.uk

Royal Botanic Gardens Kew

The Kew Royal Botanic Gardens host their tulip collection of ninety-three cultivars, which are pot grown in their Alpine Nursery and Alpine House. The recommended best time to see the tulips is throughout March and April.

https://www.kew.org/

Arundel Castle Tulip Festival, West Sussex

Founded at the end of the eleventh century by Roger de Montgomery and situated in magnificent grounds overlooking the River Arun in West Sussex, Arundel Castle Tulip Festival is the main destination to see tulips in England and quite probably, in our view, the UK, in terms of scale, breadth and endeavour. Created for the Duke and Duchess of Norfolk by their Head Gardener and the castle garden team, the Tulip Festival was highlighted as a major garden event in 2014. Further on, this amazing display has grown year on year, and it now attracts visitors from all over the UK and around the world.

In order to provide a sense of scale, it may suffice to say that for the most recent Tulip Festival, the castle

Arundel Castle is a stunning construction on its own, but when planting tens of thousands of tulip bulbs in the surrounding grounds, castle banks and gardens the scene created is nothing short of breathtaking. Tulip 'Apeldoorn' and Tulip 'Oxford' seen here have naturalised and flower successfully year on year.

garden team and volunteers planted 65,000 tulips bulbs in the autumn. Over 130 named tulips were showcased in an array of settings, including the steep castle banks, the beautiful water rill and the organic kitchen garden. In addition to offering a breathtaking display, the steep castle banks provide an excellent example of a location where tulips have perennialized, as discussed in Chapter 3. Martin Duncan, the Head Gardener at Arundel Castle, explained that the majority of bulbs in this location were planted approximately six years ago. Numbers are supplemented where necessary to ensure uniformity within the display. The Tulip Labyrinth, believed to be the first such tulip display in the world, is another great example of playful creativity that attracts and initiates interest in growing tulips for all age groups.

The tulip cake displays from the Cut Flower Garden, namely the Christening Cake and the Wedding Cake, are a somewhat unusual planted tulip feature that excites and delights visitors in equal measure; using colourful hybrids in various colour combinations, including bi-colour and single colour varieties planted close together in a pyramid fashion achieves spectacular results, which are inspiring for gardeners. A further indication of the effort and thought invested into providing visitors with a unique experience at Arundel Castle is the thatched roundhouse in the Wildflower Garden, which is surrounded by 14,000 tulips, while the Cut Flower Garden showcases an abundance of tulips throughout.

A tremendously valuable addition for gardeners interested specifically in species tulips is the unique Stumpery Garden, where the team have planted an unusual collection of delicate botanical tulips that would be expected to be found growing wild on the hillsides of Turkey, such as *turkestanica, Persian Pearl, linifolia* and *sylvestris*.

In our travels researching this book, we came to appreciate the benefits and practicalities of growing tulips in containers a lot more than we have considered this way of growing tulips in the past. If containers are,

A tulip labyrinth at Arundel Castle in West Sussex, a feature that is both inspiring and interesting.

A stunning combination of Tulip 'Claudia', Tulip 'Ballerina' and Tulip 'White Triumphator' planted in a pyramid style, is a further example of creativity by the gardeners at Arundel Castle.

for any reason, the only way to grow tulips, then Arundel Castle is the place to go in search for inspiration. With over 400 pots of tulips on display throughout the castle and landscape, featuring just about every colour and type of tulip imaginable, the examples from Arundel Castle give visitors inspiration to grow their own, no matter what size their garden or outside space is.

Over the past few years, the garden team have planted 1.2 million spring bulbs including tulips, camassia, narcissi, snake's head fritillary, scilla, alliums, hyacinths and English bluebells. As with all other destinations included in this section, and despite our focus on tulips in this book, the gardens at Arundel Castle have much to offer to visitors regardless of the season, time of year or weather on the day, but the commitment to showcase *Tulipa* as a genus in the way it is done places Arundel Castle in an unrivalled position in terms of destinations for seeing tulips.

An oversized terracotta pot superbly planted with a mix of tulips and underplanted with *Myosotis* (Forget-me-not), one of over 400 pots of tulips on display at Arundel Castle.

Brighter Blooms Tulip Open Weekend, Lancashire

Brighter Blooms Nursery is located in Walton-le-Dale, less than two miles away from Preston city centre, in Lancashire. Open usually by appointment only or on the advertised Open Days, at Brighter Blooms we follow the principle of a catalogue on the ground, where customers are able to see the tulips growing and select the varieties they wish to grow themselves. The nursery site includes a glasshouse complex, two mini-orchards, a spacious garden area with perennial borders and a large allotment. There is also a young alder coppice and a cluster of Eucalyptus trees. In the garden area and throughout the three-acre site, tulips are planted in borders, beds and containers, and a variety of temporary displays set up in a similar fashion to how we might set up displays for flower shows.

A flower show-style display created in the garden area of Brighter Blooms nursery for the annual tulip open weekend in April.

Apart from the permanent planted tulip beds, the displays are changed each year so no one open weekend is the same as the next.

We present ideas for tulip planting in different settings, and use the features available on site, with tulips and other spring bulbs planted in the coppice, sweeps of colourful tulips planted in the field and other large areas planted with tulip bulbs among the existing structures at the nursery. Most of the displays are temporary and are replaced every year when the tulip season is over, with the exception of the experimental tulip bed mentioned in Chapter 2, where the same tulip bulbs were planted six years ago and reflower every year.

The proximity to a relatively densely populated city and suburban areas means that for many of the visitors to the Brighter Blooms Tulip Open Weekend, garden space for bulb planting is often scarce. This is one of the reasons why some of our displays are on a small scale, helping gardeners visualise possibilities and tulip varieties suited to smaller gardens or backyards, and changes to space produced by the addition of colourful groups of tulips. Visitors to the event are encouraged to wander through the different parts of the site at their leisure, and to speak to staff to seek further advice and information if required. The relatively small space with the ad-hoc café becoming a focal point, gives the event the feel of a mini-festival, welcoming for gardeners and families.

TULIP GARDENS IN EUROPE

Hortus Bulborum, Limmen, The Netherlands

Situated next to the Dutch Protestant Church of Limmen, beyond the inconspicuous entrance Hortus Bulborum offers tulip lovers untold amounts of excitement, despite being a very differently set up exhibition when compared to other destinations to see tulips included in this section. Although best known for the unrivalled tulip collection, Hortus Bulborum is also home to several other spring-flowering bulb collections including crocus, daffodils, hyacinth and crown imperials (*Fritillaria*).

Hortus Bulborum, is only usually open to the public for six to eight weeks a year while tulips are in flower and is in our view both an educational resource, and a live archive at the same time. The organisation describes

Hortus Bulborum in the Netherlands is home to a vast collection of historic bulbs including tulips, narcissi and hyacinths. While it may not have the grandeur of a historic house and gardens, a visit in the spring is a must to see the breadth of tulip varieties in flower.

itself as also fulfilling the role of a gene bank for tulips. Unlike most of the other tulip destinations included in this section, at Hortus Bulborum there is little focus on creating the magic of gardens with planting of large quantities of tulips in shapes, colour combinations and scales that inspire amazement. The magic of being surrounded by colour is still there, but more importantly, the tradition of keeping systematic records of varieties is brought to life in a didactic format for the approximately 2,500 wild and cultivated tulip varieties on display here. Information cards with additional details on the tulip groups Hortus Bulborum use in their taxonomy leave very few questions unanswered.

For those interested in the history of tulips, the planted beds of individual varieties, clearly marked

Tulip 'Silver Standard' was first registered in 1760 and is one of many old varieties at Hortus Bulborum. While bulbs are not usually commercially available, the Hortus do sell off excess bulbs from time to time.

with the name and the year each variety was registered and clustered together with other varieties from the designated grouping are equally remarkable.

This impressive collection has been maintained for over eighty years, with cultivars planted in groups of affinity and it features the Rembrandt group which, under the classification used by Hortus Bulborum, includes all the flamed and feathered varieties, regardless of whether they were produced by a virus or naturally occurring. In terms of maintaining the

historical tulip collections and showcasing historical tulips to the wider public, Hortus Bulborum provides a unique and invaluable service to horticulture and history, making it a unique resource, available to anyone interested in tulips.

The compact size and well organised layout, as well as the extensive range of information available to visitors, make Hortus Bulborum a must-see destination for tulip varieties, many of which are unlikely to be seen anywhere else.

Duc van Tol Red and Yellow is the oldest tulip variety in the collection at Hortus Bulborum. Registered in 1595, it makes this variety over 400 years old!

Grand-Bigard Castle, Brussels, Belgium

Le Chateau de Grand-Bigard, or Kasteel van Groot-Bijgaarden is a hidden gem located on the outskirts of Brussels, in the Flemish Brabant region of Belgium. The very impressive twelfth century property built in the Flemish Renaissance style is surrounded by a moat and a fourteen-acre park. The castle is usually open to visitors and there you can find everything you would expect from a castle – from the courtyard, dungeon, tower, the bridge over the moat and sweeping alleys through the castle's gardens. Every spring since 2003, Grand-Bigard Castle and gardens have been home to an astonishing tulip exhibition. The scale of the tulip displays is nothing short of breathtaking, with very long swathes of planted beds of one or more tulip varieties, often following a pattern of frills or curtain swags.

Well-designed, large sweeping beds of tulips are a prominent feature in the spring at Castle Grand-Bigard.

A stunning array of tulip varieties and colours planted to great effect under the large structural trees.

Grand-Bigard Castle on the edge of Brussels is a twelfth-century castle complete with moat and is nestled in fourteen acres of park and gardens that rival Keukenhof for their tulip displays.

The colour contrasts are often bold and a never-ending source of inspiration for gardeners and designers everywhere. Every year, the planting includes standard beds of named varieties similar to varieties showcased at Keukenhof, adding an educational element to the displays. The gardens benefit from the presence of mature trees and the woodland background is put to excellent use with often very light and vivacious colour mixes, brightening up parts of the gardens and affording a joyful experience. The outstanding feature of Grand-Bigard Castle, however, is the presence of the formal planting or ornamental horticulture specific to continental Europe parks, gardens and other similar public green spaces where a splendid combination of magnitude through depth and colour enchants visitors early in the spring.

Emirgan Park Tulip Festival, Istanbul, Turkey

Given the history and the journey of the tulip bulb from Asia to Europe, through Turkey, it is unsurprising that Istanbul is home to one of world's most impressive parks and tulip festivals. Indeed, Istanbul becomes the home of the tulip throughout the month of April, with parks, gardens, public spaces and roundabouts filled with vibrant arrangements and combinations of colourful tulips.

Since 2005 the Metropolitan Municipality of Istanbul has brightened up the city every year with millions of tulips – the highest number of planted bulbs quoted being 30 million in 2016. This is arguably one of the most impressive public body-led initiatives we have come across, investing directly in aesthetics and well-being, by encouraging the population from Istanbul and much further afield to spend time outdoors enjoying the stimulation of the senses produced by the intensity of colour.

One of the most impressive parks of historical importance with vast tulip displays is Emirgan Park. Overlooking the Bosphorus Strait, the park expands across 117 acres, with discrete mini-gardens within and ample open spaces. Regardless of the season, Emirgan is an oasis of serenity, which comes to life in April every year with the most uplifting colour displays. Teams of gardeners create masterful displays of different shapes of skilfully combined colour associations. Flowing

Visitors to Emirgan Park can admire tulips with the Bosphorus Straits as a background.

Istanbul municipality ensures bright designs will be enjoyed by the visiting public at Emirgan Park.

rivers of muscari edged by yellow, red and pink tulips form a bold contrast as they sweep through wooded parts of the park.

Large flower shapes created from one or more different varieties of tulips form carpeting sections, which are further evidence of the expertise, horticultural prowess, understanding and commitment to cultural traditions and motifs as an expression of horticulture linking the past with the present. Adorning the park are three pavilions (or Köşk in Turkish), the Yellow Pavilion, the Pink Pavilion and the White Pavilion. A legacy of the Ottoman past, the pavilions are now well used by visitors to the park and integrated into leisure time as dining venues. With the spectacular background, the pavilions are a favourite spot for wedding photography.

Emirgan Park is an excellent example of a local administration taking an active role in supporting the

The impressive Yellow Pavilion in Emirgan Park, Istanbul, surrounded by mass-planted tulips.

horticulture industry, health and well-being of its residents and placing itself firmly on the must-see tulip related places worth visiting.

TULIP GARDENS ACROSS THE WORLD

Taiziwan Park, China

When thinking about China, it probably brings to mind dynamic and impressive urban development, road infrastructure and high-speed trains rather than horticultural prowess. Taiziwan Park, in Hangzhou City, Zhejiang Province, close to the eastern coast is a destination for admiring tulips that could rival any of its European counterparts.

As with all parks and gardens listed in this section, there is something to see in Taiziwan Park any time of the year. The proximity of watercourses allows for the inclusion of bridges and pavilions, and ample opportunity for relaxation and enjoyment of nature and fresh air any time of the year.

However, in early spring, usually at the end of March or beginning of April, Taiziwan Park becomes a magical place when vast displays of colourful tulips are accompanied by intense cherry blossom.

In terms of the scale of planting, there is no holding back; visually, the impact of the immense single or multi-variety planting schemes reminds visitors of the Dutch tulip fields. The colourful displays of over 300,000 tulips bring delight to the many visitors of the park. As well as having a traditional Chinese garden section, more recent developments of the park have included features such as a windmill, to complete the tulip-related picture, and a small church. These more recent additions, alongside the traditional cherry blossom background and

Taiziwan Park in China does not hold back when it comes to planting tulips for its spring displays, with 300,000 tulips planted annually.

Similar to European locations, the Chinese public are enthusiastic about tulips and Taiziwan Park is a perfect place for them to marvel at the sight of tulips.

spectacular floral displays, make Taiziwan Park a contemporary first choice for wedding photography locally.

The design and use of colour to achieve impact follows similar techniques to those applied in European gardens such as Grand-Bigard Castle, described earlier in this section, with equally remarkable results. We have included the tulip displays of Taiziwan Park in this section as a location that might come as a surprise for some. But aside from the unexpected, we wanted to highlight the effect floral displays have on everyone, regardless of where they happen to be in the world. Similarly to music, the reaction to the vibrancy and energy offered by floral displays has the same effect of awe and admiration. No common language is needed to admire floral displays; the displays are in themselves the common language.

The cherry blossom and tulip combination signals the definite arrival of spring in Taiziwan Park.

CHAPTER 7 CASE STUDY
Keukenhof

Undoubtedly the most emblematic location to see tulips, recognised worldwide, Keukenhof is located just outside Amsterdam, in the Netherlands. The aims of the exhibition, but also its association with the location

A mixed-bulb flower bed looking fantastic and admired by the crowds of people enjoying the warm spring sunshine at Keukenhof in Lisse, Netherlands.

A contemporary cut flower display of daffodils in the Oranje Nassau Pavilion at Keukenhof Gardens. Displays are changed during the eight weeks the park is open to the public.

and the symbolism that surrounds the tulip, have turned Keukenhof into a live catalogue, educational resource and tourist attraction all at the same time.

Keukenhof is a park designed on English landscape principles in the mid-nineteenth century which, since 1950, has been home to the world's biggest tulip exhibition. Independently organised and run, from the perspective of the Dutch bulb growers, Keukenhof is the platform to showcase their offering to the wider public and to forge links within the horticultural industry. From the point of view of keen gardeners, Keukenhof is a source of inspiration and knowledge, an opportunity to find out about new trends in gardening, and new varieties of tulips and other spring-flowering bulbs. For the wider public, Keukenhof is a spectacle of colour and gardening craftmanship, revolving around tulips and other spring-flowering bulbs on a scale and to a level of detail and complexity not found anywhere else.

Keukenhof covers an area of thirty-two hectares, or approximately eighty acres of parkland that includes formal gardens, a lake, woodland areas, a glasshouse complex in the centre and other pavilions that house a historic exhibition and cut flower exhibitions. The park is only open to the public for eight weeks in the spring, usually from around mid-March until mid-May, with the rest of the year being used to prepare and redesign the layout and flower beds for everything else other than the buildings and permanent vegetation, namely the 2,500 mature trees forming the canopy of the park. In terms of scale and endeavour, Keukenhof is unparalleled in the world of horticulture, with 7 million spring-flowering bulbs hand-planted every year, 4.5 million of those being tulip bulbs, in approximately 800 different varieties.

The numbers of visitors are testament to how popular Keukenhof is, with statistics showing a near doubling of visitor numbers from 884,000 to 1.5 million in less than a decade. When considering these astonishing visitor numbers, it is worth reminding ourselves that the park is only open to the public for eight weeks a year.

One of the most remarkable things about Keukenhof is that, regardless of what the weather might have been like prior to the park opening to the public, or during the mid-March to mid-May interval, visitors are guaranteed to see an incredible spectacle of colour and floral variety. The expertise and techniques available to the gardening team enable them to make changes and adjustments to the displays so that visitors have the best tulip experience possible.

Showcasing tulip varieties

Keukenhof is the perfect means for Dutch bulb growers to bring new varieties they may have on offer in front of the public. Larger beds dedicated to single tulip varieties in outdoor spaces, as well as indoor space in the Willem-Alexander glasshouse complex allow the visiting public to admire and select varieties. In some cases, the same variety can be seen at different stages of maturity. The advantage of such live catalogues is that visitors can see the tulips growing and features such as height, colour, impact can be seen at different stages of maturity, without the filters of photography and printing, which can sometimes affect the colour. Similarly, the height of the plants is often important in the context of growing conditions or design, as mentioned in Chapter 2.

The impressive displays in the Willem-Alexander glasshouse at Keukenhof are set out in blocks of different tulip varieties, which are all labelled with their names and classification groups. The displays act very much like a catalogue on the ground.

Source of inspiration and knowledge

On every occasion that we visited Keukenhof, we came across new tulip varieties or variety groups that we had been unaware of. As discussed in Chapter 4, colour mixes can be visually very impactful when planting tulips. The same can be said when mixing different types of tulips, or tulips with other spring-flowering bulbs. The success of such mixes, namely, the appropriate selection of which combinations work well, is rarely

A long tulip border among the mature trees. Getting tulip mixes to look this good requires a lot of knowledge and planning that the gardeners and designers at Keukenhof have a wealth of.

A 'drift' of *Tulipa saxatilis*, planted in a sunny opening among the trees at Keukenhof; *Tulipa saxatilis* will readily naturalise, given the correct conditions.

random, with experience and prior testing going a long way towards making a good display. At Keukenhof, the park designer works closely with the bulb growers and decides the colour mixes that will be used. This is one of the most helpful aspects in terms of inspiration and knowledge, as seeing the designs in flower and being provided with the list of varieties eliminates the testing stage for many people, thus saving time and money.

Part of the same kind of learning, design elements such as the river of *Muscari*, now considered a staple in the spring-flowering bulb display where space allows it, is the type of element much better visualised on a larger scale and adapted to the conditions available. It is also the type of idea that makes perfect sense when it can be visualised in a planted display such as that seen at Keukenhof, but despite being familiar with the plant, gardeners might not necessarily consider planting it in the style of a river.

Trends may often originate in other contexts, and garden designers are often responsible for new trends. A good example is Piet Oudolf's drift planting of Tulip clusiana 'Lady Jane' in New York, which brought a new perspective to including spring-flowering bulb planting in designs has resulted in a much wider use of drift planting of species tulips as a technique for a more naturalistic look, with some remarkable examples at Keukenhof.

Educational resource

Each year, the exhibitions – including the historical and educational exhibitions – change, and more information is added. Visitors benefit from an all-encompassing perspective, which includes a historical exhibition with facts and figures, art representations, and general information that creates the context of how long the tulip industry has existed and how it came into existence. Artefacts such as Delftware tulip single bloom vases add further to understanding the importance the tulip has in Dutch history. In itself, that is a fascinating thing to learn, but for visitors who are more practically minded and who may want to know how you go about achieving such displays, there is ample contemporaneous information including videos of the work undertaken in the park to prepare it for the following season, tools and objects associated with tulip cultivation and creating the displays in the park. There is information on the planting technique and visitors can see and handle the tools used by members of the gardening team.

Keukenhof in the Netherlands is a truly stunning garden adorned with over four million tulip bulbs in hundreds of different varieties between March and May each year, attracting over a million visitors annually.

SHOWING TULIPS IN THE UK

TULIP SHOWING FOR AMATEUR GARDENERS

Keen gardeners throughout the UK relish sharing the results of their efforts with other fellow gardeners and the general public. Quite often, that happens as part of village shows, fetes, or clubs and gardening societies' shows. More rarely, local authorities support such events, a good, more recent example being Chorley Flower Show, also touted as the 'Northern Flowerhouse'. This much-loved tradition is much more specific to the UK than any other country, with people coming together to admire and celebrate growing or baking successes as part of the community. It is also sometimes the starting point or training ground for budding horticulturalists.

The usual set-up includes categories for cut flowers, pot-grown plants, fruit, vegetables and flower arrangements, which local people can enter. Entries are judged by experts and prizes are awarded to deserving entries. Other larger scale flower shows organised by the Royal Horticultural Society (RHS) and larger horticultural societies sometimes allow for an additional class alongside professional displays, where amateurs can display and compete. Shrewsbury Flower Show organised by the Shropshire Horticultural Society, and Harrogate Flower Show organised by the

The opportunities to show tulips are not as abundant as they were at the beginning of the nineteenth century when there were hundreds of tulip shows; *Tulipa batalinii* 'Bright Gem'.

North of England Horticultural Society, both support local growing amateurs with ample space available to display the produce they have grown, the honey they have produced and their baking endeavours. However, most of these events tend to be summer events, long after the tulips have bloomed and finished flowering.

Amateur tulip displays

There are few amateur tulips shows left, with the main one being dedicated to English Florists' Tulips, organised by Wakefield and the North of England Tulips Society (WNETS), as further detailed in the case study attached to this chapter. Also in Yorkshire, the RHS has an annual tulip competition for amateurs that is held alongside the Late Daffodil competition, which takes place at the end of April or beginning of May, over the early May Bank Holiday weekend.

At the RHS Annual Tulip competition there are eighteen classes, the first being for a vase of nine tulips of one cultivar in one vase. The exhibitor whose tulips are awarded first prize also wins the Walter Blom trophy, a glass vase engraved with the recipient's name, which they keep. Of the other classes, most specify a vase of three tulips of a particular type or colour and there are also two classes for species tulips.

In recent years, the tulip competition has been held at RHS Garden Harlow Carr and, prior to the pandemic, the move north created renewed interest from exhibitors and an extra class had to be added to accommodate the number of exhibits. Interestingly, the fashion for dark-coloured flowers saw a rise in the purple and 'black' tulips being shown and the extra class was created to separate them from 'Any Other Colour' not specified in other classes. The latest innovation was to add a class for 'One vase of tulips to be judged for diversity and decorative effect', which requires additional skills from the exhibitor. Exhibitors to the Tulip Show held at RHS Garden Harlow Carr come from all age groups and walks of life, and some travel many miles with their tulips carefully packed to avoid damage. The Tulip Show is also a great opportunity for members of local gardening groups, allotmenteers, amateurs and keen gardeners to come together in their enthusiasm for tulips and the show is known for its friendly atmosphere, rather than fierce competition.

Judges Keith Eyre and his daughter, Jane Green, judge together and travel from the East Riding of Yorkshire to judge competitions from the northeast to the southern counties and are highly regarded for their fair assessment and the upkeep of traditional show standards.

Tulips in their competition vases prior to judging at the annual RHS tulip competition, held in recent years at RHS Harlow Carr Gardens.

Members of the public who visit shows are often surprised by the range of different colours, shapes and sizes of tulips seen at competitions. To see the blooms physically, as opposed to a photograph in a catalogue or a picture on screen can be a revelation; exhibition tulips are often huge and grown to perfection. The cut flowers are at eye level in vases on the show bench and the freshness, detail and occasionally the scent, are there to be enjoyed by show visitors and the wider public at close quarters. The tulip competition at RHS Garden Harlow Carr has moved from the learning centre to a large marquee in the garden. This is far more appealing and accessible to visitors and the natural light shows off the tulips far better than artificial lighting. The WNETS usually has a stand with a display of information about tulips, and there are tulip society and RHS members to answer questions and share their enthusiasm for their favourite flowers.

COMMERCIAL TULIP DISPLAYS AT FLOWER SHOWS

Professional growers, nurseries and horticultural businesses are able to demonstrate their growing expertise as part of larger and smaller flower shows. Through their displays, professional growers can introduce new varieties to the wider public and inspire gardeners and non-gardeners alike to try to grow plants they may not have tried to grow before. Furthermore, flower shows are a great opportunity to introduce the public to the breadth of varieties available commercially. As outlined at the beginning of this chapter, there are relatively fewer flower shows sufficiently early in the season to enable showcasing of tulip blooms when at their best.

In previous years, RHS Cardiff Flower Show, which used to take place in mid-April, was the ideal time of the year to display tulips at their natural flowering time. Further away in Yorkshire, the Harrogate Spring Flower Show, organised by the North of England Horticultural Society similarly early in the spring, is another one of the events where tulips are at their best and flowering is in full swing as is RHS Malvern Flower Show where bulb growers exhibit tulips, among other spring-flowering bulbs. Not last, RHS Chelsea Flower Show, which usually takes place at the end of spring, and is undisputedly the jewel in the crown of professional growers' flower shows, is an opportunity for the most masterful growers to bring tulips to the wider public.

For commercial displays at flower shows, one of the requirements that feeds into the judging criteria is the

The window for showing tulips is short; however, RHS Cardiff Flower Show was at just the right time of year for magnificent displays of tulips. A mass-planted display of tulips by Brighter Blooms.

correct labelling of the varieties on the display, with the botanical name. The judging criteria for commercial displays includes several aspects, such as the overall impression of the display, plant quality, the level of endeavour involved, with some shows including the labelling detail as a judging criterion, as mentioned above. The seasonality of the plant and how challeng-ing growing or displaying certain species out of their natural growing season is, are also aspects taken into consideration when judging.

Differing styles of displays

In this section we will consider the different types of tulip displays that growers throughout the UK contrib-ute and compete with at flowers shows. Unlike other plants, tulips can be displayed as plants in pots, in a planted garden or as cut flowers, with equally spec-tacular results. As discussed in Chapter 4, regarding design and including tulips in the garden, flower shows provide visitors with a good range of examples of ways in which tulips can be planted and the ensuing visual results for the gardens.

An example of displaying in groups of the same vari-ety, which gives a good visual understanding of how tight planting bulbs in containers might look, is given by Pheasant Acre Plants' displays. The plants to go on

display are selected for uniformity in height and flower shape, and varieties are clearly labelled, in line with requirements for RHS shows and other horticultural shows. Tulips displayed by Pheasant Acre Plants are hybrids commercially available, providing an excellent sample of the colour and shape range that gardeners and members of the public can have in their own gar-dens. As described in Chapter 4 and shown in the section dedicated for places to visit, there are several different approaches to planting tulips. Companies such as Jacques Amand International and Avon Bulbs have traditionally created more naturalistic displays in which they have included both hybrid and species tulips, alongside other spring-flowering bulbs and other perennial plants and shrubs with spectacular results.

A good example is Jacques Amand's 1995 RHS Chelsea Flower Show display, which was awarded the Lawrence Medal. This accolade is awarded annually for the best exhibit shown to the Royal Horticultural Society during the year. The scale of endeavour and inclusion of the range of tulip hybrids, as well as a vast array of other spring-flowering bulbs, herbaceous per-ennials, trees and shrubs, creating in effect a stand-alone garden is truly inspiring and well deserv-ing of the accolade.

Such displays offer show visitors interested in more unusual plants suggestions of combinations where

The versatility of tulips means that commercial exhibitors can adopt different ways of displaying tulips. Here, Pheasant Acre uses various pots to show clumps of tightly planted tulips.

tulips and other species are to be explored or discovered. In terms of colour intensity, while displays may not present the same degree of colour range as the hybrid displays, 'the understated', 'demure', 'interesting' and 'exciting' are often the best words to describe naturalistic displays.

As shown in the photo, an unexpected combination including white hybrid tulips (Tulip 'Angel's Wish'), delicate species tulips (*Tulipa tarda*), *Erythronium* 'White Beauty' interspersed with variegated *Alstroemeria* foliage, the black *Ophiopogon* foliage and berries, complete with varieties of Narcissi ranging from white (*Narcissus* 'Thalia', *Narcissus* 'White Cheerfulness') through to more intensely coloured varieties, on a bed of moss and leaf mould, make for a rich texture that reminds visitors of being in a natural environment and discovering constituent parts of the tapestry one by one.

The craft and experience demonstrated by expert growers through their displays are an open book for anyone wishing to understand the best plant companionship in terms of appearance and conditions in which they will thrive. Considered in isolation, spring-flowering plants are very attractive, but as part of

beautifully crafted combinations they become essential parts of a whole, an inspiring idea for keen gardeners and a very desirable new challenge to engage with for those gardeners who have not grown or not attempted such combinations before.

Such naturalistic spring-flowering bulb displays as those created by Jacques Amand International and Avon Bulbs fulfil an important role of knowledge-sharing, and, in many cases, act as an opportunity for the public to add to their gardening vocabulary and to expand horticultural horizons. Flower show displays created by growers existed long before the multitude of television programmes. Nonetheless, gardening programmes now play an equally important role in using expert voices to impart gardening knowledge to a vastly wider audience than flower shows can accommodate.

A different type of tulip display that can be encountered at flower shows is that where pot-grown bulbs are tightly massed together in order to showcase different varieties in a more orchestrated, theatrical set-up. In this type of display the focus is placed on colour combinations, heights and shapes, which may influence the

Mass-planted tulips in a more naturalistic setting, Jacques Amand's display at RHS Chelsea is planted to look like a garden. (Photo: Jacques Amand Intl 1995, image enhanced by Dylan Bamber, 2022)

Tulips can be associated with other spring-flowering bulbs for great naturalistic displays, as seen here in this display by Avon Bulbs.

Small pots of tulips are massed together to create a riot of colour using over twenty different varieties in this display by Brighter Blooms.

overall appearance. Brighter Blooms have adopted this particular method of display at the spring flower shows in Cardiff and Harrogate. Equally important in these types of displays are the props used to create the desired set. The choice of props may be dictated by the theme of the event, but also by the intention to provide a fla-

vour of what may be practical and what may have aesthetical value added, or what the interested public can aspire to. Garden or patio furniture is often used to create a set resembling a section of a garden or a patio. Examples such as sculptures or other such art forms included within displays or show garden design tend to

The signature style of Bloms bulbs, single varieties of cut tulip stems are massed into vases to give a visually stunning display.

be much appreciated by the public. More recently, the inclusion of vintage household items, now very much back in fashion, has repositioned gardening and garden design as a favourite pastime among younger generations, who may not have traditionally associated themselves with this hobby.

A different type of tulip display featured at some of the main RHS Shows such as the RHS Chelsea Flower Show and RHS Malvern are tulips as cut flowers, displayed in vases by Bloms. Bloms have specialised in a showing method that includes large vases set at different levels and filled with single variety cut flower tulips. Like most other commercial growers mentioned earlier in this chapter, the aim of the display is to showcase varieties that are available commercially and that gardeners can order, having seen them in flower at the show. Displaying tulips as cut flowers in clusters and with space around individual varieties allows for plants to be seen better and underlines the possibility of growing tulips in the garden for cut flowers. Visually, it also adds a degree of variation for the visiting public, and provides yet another way of visualising tulip flowers.

While flower shows are, in effect, places where tulips can be admired, we feel the aspect of showing for amateur and professional growers warrants a separate section in this book. Many gardeners and people interested in plants attend these events to gain knowledge and inspiration. For many horticultural businesses, flower shows are extremely important events in their calendars and a unique platform where growers can display their plants and answer questions related to the plants they grow.

CHAPTER 8 CASE STUDY
Wakefield and North of England Tulip Society

It is believed that at the beginning of the nineteenth century there were possibly 200 tulip shows in the UK organised yearly (Wakefield and North of England Tulip Society, 2006). There are very few remaining spring shows dedicated exclusively to tulips, with the only two we came across during the research for this book being organised by the Wakefield and North of England Tulip Society (WNETS), and RHS Harlow Carr Garden. WNETS, which appears to be the only tulip society still in existence in the UK, organises an annual show where amateur growers who are members of the society exhibit English Florists' Tulips that they have grown.

The Wakefield and North of England Tulip Society is focused on the preservation of English Florists' Tulips, as pictured here. These tulips have a more bowl-shaped flower (often described as half a tennis ball) than their Dutch counterparts.

The society – Preserving the English Florist Tulip

What sets WNETS apart in the tulip world is their focus on the English Florists' Tulips. Preserving and maintaining a collection of English Florist tulips is in fact the whole raison d'être for the society. Tulip varieties from this category are different in shape to most hybrids currently available commercially, in that the flowers are the shape of half a hollow ball. Also, the colour range for English Florists' Tulips is prescribed in three categories known as rose, bizarre and bybloemen. These three categories refer not only to the colour of the petals, but also to the colour at the base of the petal, as further detailed in our terminology box.

Once they have been affected by Tulip Breaking Virus (TBV), tulips are classed as 'broken' (or 'rectified') and are easily distinguishable because of the feathering or flaming patterns caused by the TBV. The unusual, and at the time, unexplained patterns made these tulips highly desirable during the period in Dutch history named Tulipmania, which we discuss at length in Chapter 10. Most of the English Florists' Tulips, be they breeder, feathered or flamed tulip varieties have long been unavailable commercially, but a limited stock of bulbs continues to be maintained by members of WNETS.

The availability and circulation of the English Florists' Tulip bulbs is an interesting feature of the society. Members are encouraged to pool together spare bulbs produced during the growing season, which are then distributed to other members of the society. This highly co-operative approach where

Once affected by Tulip Breaking Virus, the colours 'break' to give dramatic results. Members of WNETS maintain collections of both Breeders and Broken tulips.

resources – in this case, the bulbs – are pooled and then distributed, alongside the support, expertise and advice available from fellow members of the society may be part of the explanation for the longevity of the society.

Wakefield and North of England Tulip Society Terminology

Florist – Historically a florist was a person who grew plants for the sake of their beauty rather than for any specific other use or purpose. As time moved on, the growers who exhibited their flowers to high standards and according to specific criteria became known as florists.

English Florist Tulips – Varieties with a bowl-shaped flower often described as half a 'tennis ball'. They must have six petals and six anthers, a base colour of white or yellow and a darker main flower colour. These are split into three categories as outlined below. Varieties can exist as Breeders, Feathered or Flamed.

Breeder – These are tulips that are not visibly affected by the Tulip Breaking Virus (TBV).

Broken – Also known as 'rectified', these tulips have been infected by TBV. The virus affects the main colour of the tulip by suppressing it and allowing the base colour to become more dominant. Tulip flowers clearly showing the effects of the virus can 'break' in various ways; however, there are two distinct breaks that the society show desires: 'Flames' and 'Feathers'.

Feathered – The markings caused by TBV are confined to the outer edge of the petal, ideally in a continuous unbroken line of colour that does not stray into the centre of the petals. Good examples of feathered flowers are rare.

Flamed – In addition to the feathering around the edge of the petal, flamed flowers have a beam of rectified colour up the centre of the petals. From this beam of colour, there are fine lines of rectified colour joining to the feathering, which are separated by the base colour.

Rose – A rose breeder will have a white base colour with the petal colours of rose, scarlet, crimson or red.

Bybloemen – A bybloemen breeder will also have a white base with petal colours some shade of mauve, purple or black.

Bizarre – A bizarre breeder will have a yellow base with petal colours of orange, scarlet, brown and black. One with pink petals is unacceptable.

The Show – Preserving the English Florist Traditions

Historically, English florist societies showed their flowers in taverns and bars at a time when these were used as the main social gathering spaces, prior to village halls and community venues becoming the norm. Linked to this tradition, WNETS use single blooms presented in beer bottles as a showing method for the English Florists' Tulips. The judging criteria include the accuracy of the shape, the base colour and plant health. It must be added that as well as maintaining historical varieties, WNETS continues to adhere to the strict

An WNETS member preparing a breeder tulip for entry into the society's tulip show, held in May each year.

standards of Form, Purity and Colour, as set by the expert growers back in history known as 'florists', hence the name of English Florists' Tulips.

Alongside the historical standards which continue to be adhered to, the proceedings involved in the WNETS annual show retain the long-established associated ceremony; exhibitors arrive in the morning, and make final selections and preparations to their exhibits. At the agreed starting time, the convenor begins calling out individual categories one by one, and members step forward to add their entries on the table. A clear delineation follows each judged category, marking the different categories apart from each other and allowing visitors to easily see the entries for each category. Entries are then considered by a judging panel or a judging pair, who apply the criteria to decide the awards and feedback for entries is made available to participants. Although the judging criteria are sufficiently explicit to describe and identify perfection as regards English Florists' Tulips, the committee encourages all members to enter the Annual Show and showcase the breadth of varieties.

English Florists' Breeder Tulips are unaffected by the Tulip Breaking Virus (TBV). Tulip Solis (Breeder).

Once affected by the TBV virus, they can break in many different ways; a feathered break as pictured here will have a continuous line of colour on the edge of the petal. Tulip 'James Wild' (Feather).

WNETS use their own typology, which includes three broad categories: English Florists' Tulips, Dutch tulips and Species tulips. The Dutch tulips refer to the hybrids that are commercially available, have been cultivated, some of them for many hundreds of years, and that have not been affected by TBV. Most of the types and varieties mentioned in the other chapters of this book are likely to be Dutch tulips according to the WNETS typology. The showing method for Dutch tulips is in groups of the same variety in vases. Judging criteria for this category includes accuracy (true to type), uniformity of the blooms of the same variety within vases, and plant health. Species tulips, also referred to as Wild tulips or Botanical tulips, are acknowledged as one of the three broad categories, but they do not constitute a judged class as part of WNETS' annual show.

As tulip lovers, we think WNETS has a lot to offer in terms of making the continuation of a historical tradition possible, in terms of longevity as an amateur horticultural community, and commitment to preserving, sharing knowledge, and increasing visibility of the English Florists' Tulips, as an important part of the fascinating world of tulips. Equally, we hope readers of this book belonging to gardening groups and societies will recognise the gap in the showing and competing calendar, and will be inspired to restart local spring shows dedicated exclusively to tulips.

A break that is considered a flame will have the same continuous edge of colour as a feathered break, but will have an additional line or beam of colour in the centre of the petal that will, in turn, have fine connecting lines from it to the edge. Tulip 'Lord Stanley' (Flame).

COMMERCIAL GROWING

Most sections so far have been dedicated to information related to garden interest, gardening processes or plant growth stages in the context of general gardening. When it comes to tulips, most people start growing tulips from bulbs, the vast majority of which are produced in and exported from the Netherlands. We felt that including a chapter that provides an insight into bulb production and tulip cut flower production might be of interest to some readers and perhaps to students interested in working within the horticultural production industry. After all, without large-scale commercial production, the access to affordable tulip bulbs and cut flowers would be far more limited. Thus, in this section the focus is on production in the Netherlands, as the recognised largest exporter of tulip bulbs and tulip cut flowers worldwide.

THE DUTCH TULIP FIELDS

Bulbs, including tulips, are grown commercially in many places around the world, but no other country grows and exports the volume of tulip bulbs that the Netherlands does. A staggering three billion tulip bulbs are grown each year in the fertile Dutch soils. The 14,900 hectares of land dedicated to growing tulips

The Dutch tulip field photo is what many people visualise when they think of the Netherlands in relation to bulbs.

means that this small nation accounts for over 70 per cent of the world's production of tulip bulbs.

A hundred years ago the processes of cultivating, planting, watering, harvesting, grading, drying and counting were fundamentally the same as today, apart from the fact that the process back then was all largely carried out by people and hand tools, rather than by machines, as they are today. Following the stages of breeding, growing from seed and the creation of off-sets (or bulblets) mentioned in previous chapters, bulb growers continue the growing cycle by planting fresh bulbs, which are up to flowering size, in their fields.

Preparation and planting

The Dutch have a unique and very interesting method of ridding their fields of pests and diseases. The vast network of waterways and bunds (embankments) that exists are used to flood the fields with a few centimetres of water. The water layer stops oxygen getting into the soil and therefore pathogens harboured within are killed. This is a superbly sustainable approach that significantly cuts down on chemical usage. Once the rich sandy loam soils have been fertilised, ploughed and tilled –the equivalent of digging and raking for smaller scale growers and gardeners – the bulb growers plant offsets from the previous year's bulb harvest in October and November. By this time of year, the soils have cooled down and have fewer fungal diseases present, as discussed in Chapter 2. The bulbs are planted using large tractors and machines that have capacity to plant many thousands of bulbs in many acres of ground very quickly. Some of the machines plant the bulbs between two layers of net, which aids in the harvesting process.

Growing

The tulips' dormancy is broken by the cold winter weather and roots are followed by shoots in March. By the end of March some of the earlier varieties will be in flower and it may be that irrigation is required in the vast fields. Water is pumped from the surrounding channels and sprayed onto the crop using large watering arms that cover the width of rows, which are pulled across the land by tractors. Spraying to control aphids is usually carried out, as they are the main vector for Tulip Breaking Virus (TBV), as explained in Chapter 3. Once the tulip plants reach the flowering stage, the flower heads are all cut off, a process called 'topping'. A large tractor similar to a combine harvester is used to make this a relatively quick process; the heads are discarded between the rows of tulips to be ploughed in after the bulbs are harvested. By removing the flower heads at this stage, energy that would have otherwise gone into flower and seed production is diverted into bulb production, and the bulbs gain in size much quicker than would otherwise have been the case.

Harvest

Once the growing season is over and the foliage has died away, the bulbs can be harvested. This usually occurs around June. Machinery is used to lift the soil with the tulip bulbs; it then passes through a series of sieves, rollers and shakers to gently separate the bulbs from the soil, which is returned to the field. The bulbs are sometimes washed at this stage as well. The bulbs then go for a first or second washing at the grower's depot to remove any remaining soil so that the bulb can be seen clearly during the next stage.

Sorting, cleaning and grading

This is the part of the process that requires the largest human involvement. The bulbs pass over a conveyor

A majority of the bulbs grown in the Dutch tulip fields are destined to be used for cut flower production.

belt in front of teams of workers, who manually remove old skins and stems, rotten or damaged bulbs and other debris. The bulbs are then passed over a series of riddles that have ever-increasing sized holes with the largest bulbs dropping off the end of the machine. This grades the bulbs into the requisite sizes, such as 9–10cm (3½–4in), 10–11cm (4–4½in) and 12cm+ (5in+). These sizes refer to the circumference of the bulb rather than the diameter; a bulb with an 12cm (5in+) diameter will not have been able to fall through the smaller holes at the beginning of the machine but will drop through the holes greater than 12cm (5in+), grading it as a 12cm+ (5in+) bulb. The smaller offsets and bulbs will be stored for replanting in the autumn.

Drying and storing

The bulbs are placed in large pallet crates that allow for air to be blown through them so that the bulbs are thoroughly dried out. They are then stored in warm temperatures and constantly checked for excess humidity, which is controlled by good air flow. The bulbs are then distributed to the wholesalers for packing, or stored until the cut flower growers are ready to plant the next crop.

Some of our readers may be surprised to learn that the smallest proportion of the bulbs end up in garden centres and mail order companies for sale as dry bulbs to the public. It is the tulip cut flower industry that accounts for the largest proportion of tulip bulbs grown in the Netherlands, with at least 60 per cent of all bulbs grown used in this sector.

FORCING TULIPS FOR THE CUT FLOWER MARKET

The cut flower industry is a significant worldwide industry, growing millions of stems of different flowers twelve months of the year. When we look specifically at tulips, the focus of the growing of cut flowers once again falls to the Dutch. Most of the tulips grown in the Netherlands are grown using the method of forcing. Most of the longer stemmed tulips varieties naturally flower from mid-April to mid-May; it is possible to manipulate these varieties into flowering as early as November. This is where the term 'forcing' comes from, literally meaning that bulbs are forced to flower early. While this may sound like an easy process, many years of trial and error, and research and development over the previous decades have contributed to the Dutch cut flower industry becoming what it is today.

Traditionally, like other flowers, tulips were grown in the ground in open fields and were cut as they became ready. Flowers grown in this way tend to have larger flower heads and sturdier stems; however, there is no controlling the weather and both quality and timings can be wildly affected. On a small scale, this approach

To grow the perfect bloom, large glasshouses allow growers to control the environment to a greater degree than if they were growing outside.

can be made to work well but demand can soon out-strip supply, or potentially the opposite can happen, with lots of tulips out in flower when the crop is ready, and poor demand. The latter has certainly helped to drive the growing of tulips as cut flowers out of their natural season. By forcing tulips into flower out of season, key dates in the calendar such as International Women's Day, Easter and potentially even Christmas, can be catered for with tulips as cut flowers.

In a bid to better control growing conditions, cut flower tulip growing moved into glasshouses, where it was soon discovered that flowering could be achieved much earlier. However, as mentioned in earlier chapters, tulips require a period of cold to root and grow properly. If they do not get a long enough and cold enough period of cold, the bulbs will not grow properly, the stems will not elongate and flower buds may fail. To get round this problem, tulip bulbs are pre-chilled in large cold stores before planting, this method emulating a cold season and initiating the growing stages. Growing tulips in the ground in glasshouses was replaced by growing tulips on raised benches in trays of soil or special growing media. Having tulips growing at waist height improved efficiencies and the ergonomic aspects that concern the workforce in this industry, especially for the stage of cutting the flowers, saving workers the need for unnecessary additional bending when picking and cutting. For the past two decades, mass-produced cut flower tulips have been grown almost exclusively hydroponically. Hydroponics is a technique used to grow plants in a nutrient solution, eradicating the need for heavy soil-based systems. By growing in water, everything the tulip needs to grow perfectly (nutrients, pH and water temperature) can be controlled very carefully; tulips grown hydroponically also grow quicker and more evenly. It might seem that this system uses a lot of water, but in reality it actually uses less than a traditional soil-based system would require, as the water is recirculated in a closed loop.

The Dutch horticulture industry has always been ahead of many other countries in terms of its innovative approach, situating the Netherlands as undisputed world leaders in horticulture. They have streamlined the process of forcing a cut tulip flower into an almost factory-like process with vast glasshouses spanning many acres full of automation and even robotics. The largest of these nurseries are forcing 100 million tulip stems per year.

COMMERCIAL GROWING IN THE UK

A combination of excellent growing conditions in the Netherlands, coupled with heavy investment in bulb production have resulted in the Netherlands becoming very competitive in producing and supplying tulip bulbs worldwide. In the UK, tulip bulb production has

Flowers from the Farm (FFTF) is a movement that focuses on small scale, artisan, locally grown cut flower production.

dwindled significantly in the past few decades, with only one larger scale tulip bulb producer we have been able to identify in the UK, based in the Norfolk area. The bulbs produced in Norfolk are destined nearly exclusively for growing as cut flowers.

Flowers from the farm – commercial cut flower growing?

It would be remiss of us while talking about the advances and developments in growing tulips for cut flowers and for bulb production on an industrial scale, not to mention the fact that the last decade had seen a significantly increased interest in British-grown cut flowers, and the growth of the 'Flowers from the Farm' (FFTF) movement.

Environmental concerns linked to cut flower transport and the associated greenhouse emissions, alongside the desire to support small enterprise and artisan growers and traditional field-growing methods, akin to traditional gardening, has meant that in specific locations throughout the UK there is more availability of British-grown tulips alongside other flower varieties. One such artisan grower is Bayntun Flowers, as mentioned in Chapter 7. FFTF is a different approach to producing cut flowers, appreciated by customers with an interest in the environmental aspects of growing.

CHAPTER 9 CASE STUDY
A small tulip grower for cut flowers in the Netherlands Q&A

During our last trip to the Netherlands we sat down with Adriaan Dekker, the owner of Maatschap Dekker-Mol, one of the smaller cut flower producers from the province of North Holland, who agreed to share facts and figures on growing cut flower tulips.

Question: How many tulip flowers do you grow and when?

The company forces five million stems between November and mid-April. All the growing takes place in glasshouses that can be heated or cooled to maintain perfect growing temperatures. That seemed like a large number to us, but Adriaan explained that it is quite a small number, with many tulip forcers growing well over twenty million stems. He believes that his company is growing the minimum amount in order to be commercially viable within the industry.

Question: How can you be competitive when others have the advantage of increased scale?

Adriaan explained how, in his company, they take a slightly different approach: because they only grow a few million stems, that allows them the time to also plant, grow and harvest a majority of their own tulip bulbs, whereas the larger growers tend to buy in most of the bulbs they will be growing as cut flowers. The company has been operating this way now for many years so something must be working correctly.

Question: Can you guide us through the process of forcing a tulip?

Tulip bulbs that have been stored are placed onto spikes in pin-trays (a plastic tray that has lines of sharp points inside). The trays are then filled with water, so the base of the bulb is submerged. The trays are stacked on pallets and taken into the cold store. Once they have been there for two or three weeks, they

Tulip bulbs are placed close together onto spikes in the bottom of the pin tray. They grow to be fully formed plants in a matter of weeks.

have made lots of white roots and are starting to shoot. The trays are then placed onto the benches in the glasshouse and allowed to grow. All the benches move around the glasshouse and by the time they arrive at the front they have grown and are ready for cutting.

Question: How long does that whole process take?

From placing the bulbs into the trays to bunching the stems ready for supermarkets or flower markets takes approximately five to six weeks, so it is quite a quick process. It means that Adriaan and his workers can get a few different crops through the glasshouse in a growing season.

Question: We understand that the tulip forcing industry is highly mechanised; is there a stage where people are more involved in the process?

The process of collecting and bunching of the tulips involves the most amount of people. The workers take the stem with the bulb from the pin trays and place them on a conveyor belt. The bulb

A tulip plant pulled from the pin tray after five to six weeks of growing. Healthy white roots can be seen.

is cut off automatically, after which the stems are weighed to make sure they meet a certain set of criteria. A machine counts them into bunches and automatically ties them. A worker then takes the smaller bunches and wraps them together in one large bunch, which they place in buckets and onto trollies ready to be transported to their point of sale.

Bunches of cut tulip stems after grading, counting and banding.

The tulip bud is formed but not yet coloured. A worker can be seen pulling the stems complete with bulbs out of the trays to be placed onto a conveyor belt for cutting.

Bunches are wrapped together in paper to stop them bending and placed in buckets of water. From here they will go to their point of sale.

Question: What does a tulip forcer do in his spare time?

They breed tulips, of course! Adriaan showed us his small collection of tulip seedlings that have been grown from seed that he has collected from crosses made in previous years.

A vase of cut flowers, Tulip 'Uncle Tom' (Double Late).

CHAPTER 10

TULIP HISTORY

Including the history chapter at the very end of this book might seem somewhat counterintuitive. We think the history of the tulip is entirely enthralling. However, this book is intended as a practical guide and focuses on cultivation and lessons learnt from our experience of growing tulips. With an anticipated audience comprising mainly keen gardeners, horticulture students and people generally interested in growing tulips, we felt that the history of tulips must be included, albeit not as the opening gambit. During our research for this chapter, we found extensive material and more nuanced interpretations of what pertains to the history of tulips, which are rarely given attention. We invite readers to further explore the fantastic accounts eloquently put forward by historians we reference in this chapter. For our part, we will use this chapter to present a short synopsis of the history and to bring to the fore more recent interpretations and new thinking;

Hortus Bulborum maintains a collection of many of the old varieties of tulips, which are largely unavailable to the public today.

this, in turn, brings into question if reporting of the facts across centuries has engendered a 'Chinese whispers' effect, which might have distorted reality.

The history of the tulip is vast and convoluted and a short chapter here cannot delve completely into all its nooks and crannies. Most readers will have heard the term 'Tulipmania', which is the most talked-about period in the history of tulips. But much happened before that short and intense period and much more has happened since. In fact, some scholars now question if the Tulipmania period has been incorrectly reported and interpreted. Recent research is starting to shed new light and change our understanding of the period.

The spread of the tulip from its eastern origins can be traced as it was transported along the east to west trade routes and conquests of days long ago, finally arriving in Western Europe in the late 1500s after a 500-year-long journey.

TULIP ORIGINS

As explored in Chapter 1, the tulip is not a native of Western Europe; it originates from the Tien Shan and Pamir-Alay mountain ranges in Central Asia. Islamabad acts as a good pinpoint on the map for those wishing to visualise a location. Taxonomists tend to agree that the tulip most likely came into existence in and around these mountain ranges, but when they appeared we are not entirely sure.

We know that by 1050, in Persia, the tulip had made the jump from being a wild mountain bulb to a flow-ering garden plant that was admired and widely grown for its attractive colours and forms. The gardens of the Persian capital, now known as Baghdad, were well established and contained collections of tulips.

Nomadic Turks roamed the foothills of these mountains shepherding their flocks around this time. They were also familiar with the tulip from their wandering through the mountains. As time went on, these hardened people start to travel westwards, away from their isolated rural Persian beginnings. They started to settle in towns, becoming far less nomadic and their travels become one of plundering, settling cities and further expanding their lands and creating a dynasty, which was to become the Ottoman Empire. It is unclear what the status of tulips was at this point, but what is known is that gardens were revered, and flowers were considered sacred.

By 1345 the Ottomans had reached the edge of Europe and were looking toward Constantinople as the new centre for the empire. A few setbacks meant it took over half a century until the Turks sieged and conquered Constantinople, immediately changing its name to Istanbul. With the new geographic and administrative settlement as the centre of the empire, a new home for the tulip came about. There was now impetus to create gardens and public spaces in which many plants, including the tulip, could be showcased. A relatively settled period established itself under the Ottoman rule, overseen by a string of fierce sultans. Sultans were well educated, cultured and religious men who enjoyed gardening.

TURKEY AND THE OTTOMAN EMPIRE

Records show that the tulip was cultivated in Turkey from as early as 1000AD. Before this time, only a single wild tulip variety is known. However, the tulip really starts to flourish during the stability brought about by the conquest of Constantinople by Suleiman the Conqueror in 1453. Large palaces and vast gardens were created by the Ottomans over the next 100 years. The gardens were seen as a retreat from the busy and brutal lives that many of the rulers led, and were considered to be a heaven on earth. The Muslim faith tells Ottomans that heaven will be a paradise

A tulip growing in its more natural settings among the foothills of the mountains. The tulip is not native to Western Europe, but has travelled here via a long history.

Approximate extent of the Ottoman
Empire in mid 17th century ---------

The pink shaded area on the map shows the large area that the Ottoman Empire had conquered by the middle of the seventeenth century. The proximity of their northwestern border with Europe allowed for trade and diplomatic relations to be fostered, and tulips were brought to Western Europe this way. The Tien Shan mountain range is noted for reference as the area with the largest native diversity and the starting point for the history of the tulip.

garden. They were very accomplished horticultural-ists, and many plants were grown in their gardens from fruit to flowers, including many types of bulbs. Tulips, however, quickly became hugely popular and were grown widely, with sultans importing vast quan-tities of bulbs from the east. By 1520, the grandson of Suleiman the Conqueror, Suleiman II or Suleiman the Great was in power and the empire was stronger than ever. He was a fanatical horticulturist and his passion for the tulip led to the first changes in flower shape, colour and size. Essentially, the first selective breed-ing for certain traits was conducted under his supervision.

Up until this point in the Turks' history, idolising things for use as symbols and motifs had been frowned upon for religious reasons. But views and times were changing, and the tulip became the motif of choice. Many paintings, tiles, vases and items of clothing have been discovered adorned with tulip motifs. What we can see from these items is that the Ottomans coveted a very different-shaped tulip flower to the rounded cup shape that is considered the norm today. The longer and thinner the petal, the better – the ultimate goal was almost needle-like. As many as 1,500 new varieties were bred under Suleiman's careful watch, and they became known as the Istanbul Tulips. Tulip growing, collecting and breeding continued apace in Turkey

The sultans of the Ottoman Empire were fearless leaders, but when not plundering and fighting, they were avid gardeners. They cultivated many plants, but tulips were one of their favourites.

Tulipa acuminata is the closest tulip type and form favoured by the Ottoman sultans that remains cultivated today. The more needle-like the petals, the better.

We are so familiar with tulips today that it is hard to believe that, until the mid-sixteenth century, the tulip was a completely unfamiliar flower in Western Europe. Once it arrived, it quickly gained popularity.

Tulip motifs were used to adorned tiles, vases and painting in seventeenth-century Turkey.

under the Ottomans over the next few hundred years. However, by the mid-1500s the tulip travelled the next leg of its journey into Western Europe.

Even during these relatively settled times, the Ottoman sultans were a force, and not one to cross. In a bid to avoid fighting the Turks, Europeans began to travel more frequently to Turkey to forge diplomatic relationships. The tulip, a flower not seen before in Western Europe, did not go unnoticed.

INTRODUCTION INTO WESTERN EUROPE

European botanists did not start to mention the tulip until the mid-sixteenth century. Prior to this, the tulip was largely unknown, or at least undocumented in Western Europe. There are many stories and theories as to how the tulip first arrived in Western Europe.

Many of them cannot be verified, nor can we pinpoint the arrival down to one specific point in time, as tulip bulbs probably arrived at multiple destinations in Europe over a period of years. There is one particular story that has been retold time and time again and is often cited as the factual account of the tulip's entry into Europe, although parts of it are difficult to verify and there are some suggestions that elements are unlikely to be completely factual. However, it is one of our favourite tales and we feel it is worth telling here.

Ogier Ghiselin de Busbecq (1522–1591) was one of the many diplomats moving between Europe and Turkey in a quest to better understand the Ottomans' culture and traditions, and therefore improve relations with the fearsome neighbour. He was employed by the Emperor Ferdinand I of the Habsburg Empire (parts of which are now Austria and Germany), as letter writer and ambassador to Suleiman II in Istanbul. He wrote many letters back to Ferdinand describing people, places and every-

When Carolus finally moved to Hortus Botanicus in Leiden in 1593, to take up a professor position, it gave him a permanent place to plant his ever-increasing tulip collection. Pictured: the Clusius Garden today.

Carolus Clusius (1526–1609) played an important role in the spread of the tulip into and around Western Europe. He was a prolific letter writer and often included tulip bulbs with his postings.

thing in between. He was a keen botanist in his own right, and many of his letters have descriptions of flowers and plants, and it is these that are of most interest. He first saw the tulips in flower on his travels to Istanbul in 1554 and his letters clearly show 'surprise' on seeing these 'new' flowers. During his time in Istanbul, Busbecq sent both seeds and bulbs back to Europe, which were planted in the gardens in Vienna and tulips flowered for the first time in Europe. This is how the story was told, but it is now believed that letters that make up a book of letters were written at a much later date, possibly as late as the 1580s. This and other inconsistencies sow doubt into the exact fact of this tale. Undoubtably, Busbecq did send bulbs back to Europe, but quite when we cannot be sure. There are many other accounts of the tulip flowering the first time in Europe. *The Tulip* by Anna

Pavord and *Tulipomania* by Mike Dash elegantly recount some of these stories and both are worth reading for a greater understanding.

We know that Busbecq sent tulip bulbs back to his good friend Carolus Clusius in 1572, who was living and working in Vienna, establishing an imperial botanical garden. Clusius was already familiar with the tulip, by this time having first seen tulips flowering in a friend's garden in Antwerp sometime between 1564 and 1568. Clusius was an avid letter writer and corresponded widely with horticulturalists, botanists and friends around Europe. He would often send bulbs of various types, including tulip bulbs, with his letters and he certainly helped to spread the tulip across Western Europe. He spent many years away in various locations across Europe studying and writing about plants. By the mid-1570s Clusius is renowned as one of the top botanists in Europe. This, combined with his letter writing and bulb sending, makes him pivotal in the spread of the tulip across Europe.

In 1593, already an old man by then, he moved to Leiden in the newly formed United Provinces of the Netherlands (what we broadly call the Netherlands today), to take up a professorship post and establish a botanical garden at the new university. Clusius was instrumental in the first attempt at a classification system of tulips, noting differences between flower shape and flowering time. His new job at the university gave him the chance to consolidate his life's work. It also allowed him to plant his extensive collection of tulip bulbs in the fertile Dutch soils.

By the early 1600s, tulips had become more well known among gardeners and many new varieties had been raised by the skilled horticulturalists of the time. This still relatively 'new' flower started to attract the attention of many people from all different backgrounds right across Europe, but it seems nowhere else quite as much as in the Netherlands. It is believed that tulips reached England around 1582.

TULIPMANIA

The period most frequently referred to as 'Tulipmania' occurred in the Netherlands and spans a period of about four years, culminating in a frenzied peak in 1637. However, factors in the previous thirty years contributed to the tulip's rise to fame and helped to set the scene for mania to occur. The usual story of

Tulipmania follows the general lines that a new wondrous flower caught the attention of the Dutch population right from the wealthiest nobles down to the poorest commoners. They all started to buy as many tulip bulbs as they could afford, and some sold them on. A speculative frenzy occurred where bulbs were reportedly sold on as many as ten times in a single day. The prices were pushed up to dizzying heights by the huge demand and then, almost overnight, in 1637 the market crashed and the bulbs became almost worthless. This led to people losing homes and livelihoods and shook the country's economy so severely that the Dutch government was required to step in and bail people out of bankruptcy. In reality, this is quite a simplistic view of what was going on at the time. While it may be that some of the stories do not appear to be based on hard evidence, there is no space or scope in this chapter to delve too deeply into it all.

What is evident is that a rise in the prices of tulip bulbs did happen, and there were buyers who spent

A large collection like this in the early 1600s would have cost a vast sum of money and would only be available to the wealthy.

Tulips in the 1600s tended to be admired for the beauty of a single bloom rather than the modern fashion of large bouquets. Vases like this were designed to allow individual blooms to be appreciated.

A historic group of single tulips with distinct colours, these tulips were referred to as 'Breeder Tulips', a group that is all but extinct, apart from a few small private collections. They are late flowering, often as late as mid-May.

large sums of money on tulip bulbs in the early 1600s. There was a sudden fall in prices that will have caused financial damage and quite possibly impacted negatively on the livelihoods of some. Did this rock the Dutch economy to such a calamitous extent? Probably not. There are many factors that come together that allowed this speculative craze to happen, and once again for a broader and deeper understanding of these factors, the two books mentioned earlier in the chapter are well worth a read.

It is worth noting that the Netherlands in this period was going through a golden age generally. The country was settled by the uniting of the provinces and had established the Dutch East India Company. Merchants and traders flocked to the country; its sea connections allowed the Netherlands to become a commercially

important hub within Europe and as such, it prospered. The Netherlands at this time became one of the wealthiest nations in Europe. The country was also undergoing social transformation that allowed for a greater appreciation of material 'things', and there were many people (mainly men) who had amassed great fortunes. With their fortunes came the ability to build large homes and furnish them lavishly with the latest fashions of the era. This naturally extended to the gardens. Having a large garden to show off the latest plant imports had become a must for the well-heeled nobles, businessmen and merchants of the day. Within the garden plenty of space was made for the latest fashionable plant, the tulip. Beds were set aside just for tulips and some gardeners planted many hundreds or thousands of bulbs. But it was only the very rich that could afford to obtain a large collection of the most popular varieties.

The feathered or broken tulips were the truly sought-after varieties, as opposed to the solid-coloured tulips, referred to as 'breeder tulips' back then. Back in Chapter 3 we looked at the Tulip Breaking Virus (TBV) and how it changes a solid-coloured tulip into one with mottled or feathered patterns on the petals. The unique colours and patterns that appeared on these tulips were a large part of what pushed this flower to the forefront. In the seventeenth century there was no understanding of viruses and there would not be for nearly a further 300 years. The horticulturalists of the time had no way of knowing that the virus was transmitted by aphids and that they would not be able to break a tulip colour by any other method. Feathering on some of today's tulip varieties is the result of stable mutations or specific breeding, not the result of a virus. Back in the seventeenth century it was not understood why the bulbs of a broken tulip got weaker over time, even with immaculate care and attention, or why few or no offsets were produced. All these things helped to increase the allure of these unusually marked flowers. By the very nature of their rarity and randomness, the broken tulips fetched the highest prices. The most well-known variety that gets mentioned most in documents and articles is Tulip 'Semper Augustus'. This variety is famed for being the most expensive tulip bulb ever sold. Factual evidence is difficult to come by, but there are reports that a single bulb of this variety sold for somewhere between 5,000 and 10,000 guilders at the height of Tulipmania. That would have bought a very nice houseboat on a canal in

Tulip 'Semper Augustus' is one of the most well-known broken tulips from the Tulipmania period, with a single bulb allegedly selling for the same price as a well-appointed houseboat in the centre of Amsterdam.

Tulip 'Silver Standard' is a good example of the type of tulip that commanded the highest prices during Tulipmania. It is, however, a naturally bred Single Early variety dating from 1760 that is unaffected by Tulip Breaking Virus.

the centre of Amsterdam at the time, and equated to over ten times the salary of a skilled tradesman. Noticeable other varieties are Tulip 'Viceroy' and Tulip 'Admiral van der Eijck', and all have finely feathered patterns on their petals.

Even in skilled gardeners' hands, there were still not that many bulbs available. They were still learning the best way to propagate and bulk the bulbs up, and it was proving a slow process. Combined with the effect of the virus weakening the mother bulbs and reducing the production of offsets, and the tulip becoming more fashionable and sought-after, demand soon started to outstrip supply. Even with professional growers starting nurseries dedicated to growing bulbs, the demand for certain varieties could not be met in the mania years.

In the early 1600s most of the tulip buying and selling was still conducted directly between gardeners,

Tulip 'Viceroy' is listed in 1637 Dutch tulip catalogue at between 3,000 and 4,200 guilders, around ten times the yearly salary of a skilled craftsman at the time.

who obviously had a passion for growing in general. Even as tulips became more fashionable in the 1610s and the 1620s and the rich entered the market, they were still buying the bulbs to add to their gardens. These were connoisseurs who were buying tulips for the sake of having the bulbs, and the thought of buying just to sell them immediately on to the next person had yet to occur.

What really seems to have pushed the buying and selling to the next level is the establishment of so-called 'florists', who started to buy tulip bulbs with the only intention of selling them on again. There were many taverns in the Netherlands at the time and they were as good a place as any to hold meetings and conduct trade. This appears to be where a lot of the tulip trading happened. There was a stock market established and based in Amsterdam, but tulip bulbs were never traded there. Maybe the easy access via the taverns or the stories of large sums of money made overnight, or the fashion within high society, caused people who had never owned a garden, let alone planted tulips before, to enter the bulb buying market – most probably it was a combination of all these factors. While a few of the connoisseurs did frequent the taverns and participate in these trades, it was mainly those with lesser means. This helped to set up some of the future financial problems, as it became commonplace

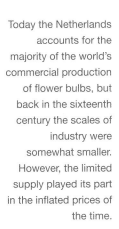

Today the Netherlands accounts for the majority of the world's commercial production of flower bulbs, but back in the sixteenth century the scales of industry were somewhat smaller. However, the limited supply played its part in the inflated prices of the time.

for buyers to purchase bulbs with both money (what little they had) and goods – anything from a cow to a piece of furniture. Until now tulip buying had always been conducted during the time the bulbs were lifted from the ground, hence there was a reliable stock. Now the trading was conducted at all times of the year, so bulbs could not be inspected at the time of sale and, in most cases, trust had to be put in a note stating what was being sold. So rather than pay in full for the bulbs, it became customary to place a deposit with a promise to pay the remainder by a certain date when it was established the bulbs were true to name. This helped to free up capital to trade on other bulbs. It also meant that most sellers had the majority of their predicted profits tied up in various, often complicated, chains of transactions and deals.

The prices paid for the tulips climbed steadily during the years 1634–1636 and reached their peak towards the end of 1636 and the beginning of 1637. The prices reached a point where they were so high that uncertainty crept into the market as to whether they could go any higher. Some of the wary traders decided they would not pay the high prices and fairly quickly no one was buying, and therefore no one could sell. The complicated sales chains quickly broke down and if one buyer in the chain could not pay, it usually meant that the previous seller could also not fulfil his debt, leading to the whole chain of debt to collapse. While people certainly lost money, there was never a significant amount of physical money in circulation, and most probably lost money they never had in the first place. In the end, a lot of debt was written off and traders ended up with the original deposit if they were lucky. Most traders went back to their previous profession where they could. Many of the connoisseurs and those with lots of money and large gardens were unlikely to be seriously impacted financially. For traders and connoisseurs alike, it was more the breaking of promises and the breaking down of societal norms that was most problematic.

CURRENT THINKING

The further we go back in history, the harder it becomes to find reliable evidence. Especially as regards plants, they were not documented in the same

Newly-gained wealth from tulip sales did not always sit easy with all the Dutch population during the 1600s. This satirical painting uses monkeys to depict the antics of the Dutch tulip traders.

Tulip 'Duc van Tol Red and Yellow' is the oldest tulip variety still in cultivation at Hortus Bulborum; it dates from 1595.

way as battles, reigning monarchs or scholars. Prior to the sixteenth and seventeenth centuries when the Western world started to take a real interest in biology and the happenings of the world, information on animals and plants was gleaned from historical evidence that happened to mention the tulip being grown or cultivated. As and when studies are conducted today, new information sometimes emerges that sheds new or differing light on things. For example, there is some recent research from the University of Cordoba and the School of Arabic Studies in Spain that speculates that the tulip could have arrived in the Netherlands much earlier than is currently understood. While they cannot categorically prove it, they provide solid evidence to support a hypothesis that the tulip arrived in Holland via Spain up to five centuries earlier than the 1600s.

Trying to untangle stories, myths, propaganda and misinformation about the tulip's history and, in particular,

Tulip 'Duc van Tol Orange' dates from 1700 and 'Duc van Tol Scarlet' from 1850. The complete 'Duc van Tol' collection at Hortus Bulborum contains twenty-two different cultivars.

Tulipmania, has been attempted over the years, but not as often as one might think. Many of the retold stories around Tulipmania are based on previous accounts, which have often not been fact checked.

Satirical pamphlets ridiculing the exploits of the tulip sellers and buyers at the time are an example of this. The Netherlands was going through a golden age at the time of Tulipmania, and had become one of the richest countries in Europe. This newfound wealth did not always sit easily with a proportion of the Dutch population, the majority of whom were quite religious. This proportion of the population would print leaflets to advertise to the rest how ungodly it was to speculate on the tulip. Some of the stories told today may have been based on these leaflets, and it would be fair to question the level of bias of their authors.

Anna Goldgar's book *Tulipmania: Money, Honor, and Knowledge in the Dutch Golden Age* is the most recent body of work to really try and untangle some of the myths and stories. Goldgar extensively scoured and researched source material mostly in the Netherlands, with the aim to unearth factual evidence to back up the stories that have been told for hundreds of years. What Godgar found was evidence of increasing prices, speculative gain and falling prices, but little to prove that Tulipmania was as large a speculative frenzy or massive financial crash that we credit it with today. The book really sheds light on the economic transitions in the Netherlands and the social insecurities the Dutch people were going through at the time.

There is much interest and fascination in Tulipmania as a story because of the parallels in the more recent financial history; in themselves, two fields that apparently can have no connection to each other – financial speculation and new tulip varieties. Yet Tulipmania is the background and combines the two discrete fields in a way that explores and exposes some human traits that have remained unchanged. Whether or not the 'real and complete history' of Tulipmania will ever be uncovered, only time will tell. Certainly, the stories are as colourful as the tulips themselves and make for tales that will endure.

BIBLIOGRAPHY

Akers, J. *et al. Flames and Feathers: English Florists' Tulips* Wakefield and North of England Tulip Society (Charlesworth Press, 2012)

Amsterdam Tulip Museum, www.amsterdamtulipmuseumonline.com

Baker, C. & Lemmers, W. *Tulipa: A Photographer's Botanical* (Artisan, Workman Publishing, 1999)

Bermejo, H., Esteban, J. & Sánchez, G. *'Tulips: An Ornamental Crop in the Andalusian Middle Ages* (Economic Botany 63(1), 2009, pp.60–66)

Breed, E. *Going Wild for Tulips* (Self published, date unknown)

Centraal Bureau voor de Statistieken (CBS), *Hectares of Tulips Grown* (2021)

Conijn, C. *Tulip diseases shown for each growth stage* (Roodbont Publishers, 2017)

Dash, M. *Tulipomania: The Story of the World's Most Coveted Flower and the Extraordinary Passions it Aroused* (Weidenfeld & Nicolson, 1999)

Denton, J.O. & Denton, G.J. 'First report of *Ilyonectria* sp. affecting foliage of *Tulipa*' (*New Disease Reports* **29**, 23, 2014)

Dongen, R.V. *The Tulip Anthology* (Chronicle Books, 2010)

D W Design *Tulip book: Information and picture together* (D W Design)

Englemann, J. & Hamacher, J. *Encyclopedia of Virology* (Academic Press, third edition, 2008)

Goldgar, A. *Tulipmania: Money, Honor, and Knowledge in the Dutch Golden Age* (The University of Chicago Press, 2008)

Integrated Pest Management (IPM), *Reports on Plant Diseases: Tulip Fire or Botrytis Blight* (illinois.edu)

King, M. *Gardening with Tulips* (Frances Lincoln, 2005)

Li, Y., Chen, L., Zhan, X., Liu, L., Feng, F., Guo, Z., Wang, D. & Chen, H. 2022. *Biological effects of gamma-ray radiation on tulip (Tulipa gesneriana* L.). *PeerJ* 10:e12792 DOI 10.7717/peerj.12792

Maarten, J.M. et al. 'Tiptoe through the tulips – cultural history, molecular phylogenetics and classification of *Tulipa* (Liliaceae)', (*Botanical Journal of The Linnean Society*, 2013, vol.172, pp.280–328)

Mahy, B.W.H. & van Regenmortel, M.H.V. *Desk Encyclopedia of Plant and Fungal Virology, first edition. Chapter: Plant virus diseases: Ornamental plants* (Elsevier, Academic Press, 2009, pp.207–229)

Miller, B. 'Tulip planting depth in the landscape', *Royal Anthos, Research Newsletter No. 42*, (Cornell University, February 2019)

Moore, R., Clark, W.D. & Vodopich, D.S. *Botany, second edition* (WCB/McGraw-Hill, 1998)

Neefjes, H. *Tulip propagation breakthrough* (www.hortipoint.nl/floribusiness/tulip-propagation-breakthrough/ 2018)

Pavord, A. *The Tulip* (Bloomsbury Publishing, 2000)

Rees, A.R. & Turquand, E.D. *'Effects of planting density on bulb yield in the tulip', Journal of Applied Ecology,* (British Ecological Society, vol.6, No. 2 (Aug, 1969), pp.349–358)

Royal General Bulb Growers' Society (KAVB) *Classified List and International Register of Tulip Names* (1971 edition)

Royal General Bulb Growers' Society (KAVB) *Classified List and International Register of Tulip Names* (Editor J. van Scheepen, 1996 edition)

SFGATE *Are Tulips Heliotropic & Photonastic?* (https://homeguides.sfgate.com/tulips-heliotropic-photonastic-98246.html, Nov 2021)

Statista www.statista.com

Wakefield and North of England Tulip Society http://www.tulipsociety.co.uk/ (2022)

Wilford, R. *Tulips: Species and Hybrids for the Gardener* (Timber Press, 2006)

Wilford, R. *The Plant Lover's Guide to Tulips* (Timber Press, 2015)

ABBREVIATIONS

TBV – Tulip Breaking Virus

RHS – Royal Horticultural Society

WNETS – Wakefield and North of England Tulip Society

KAVB – Koninklijke Algemeene Vereeniging voor Bloembollencultuur; translated as Royal General Bulb Growers' Association

FFTF – Flowers from the Farm

INDEX

A page number in **bold** denotes a photograph of the subject is shown